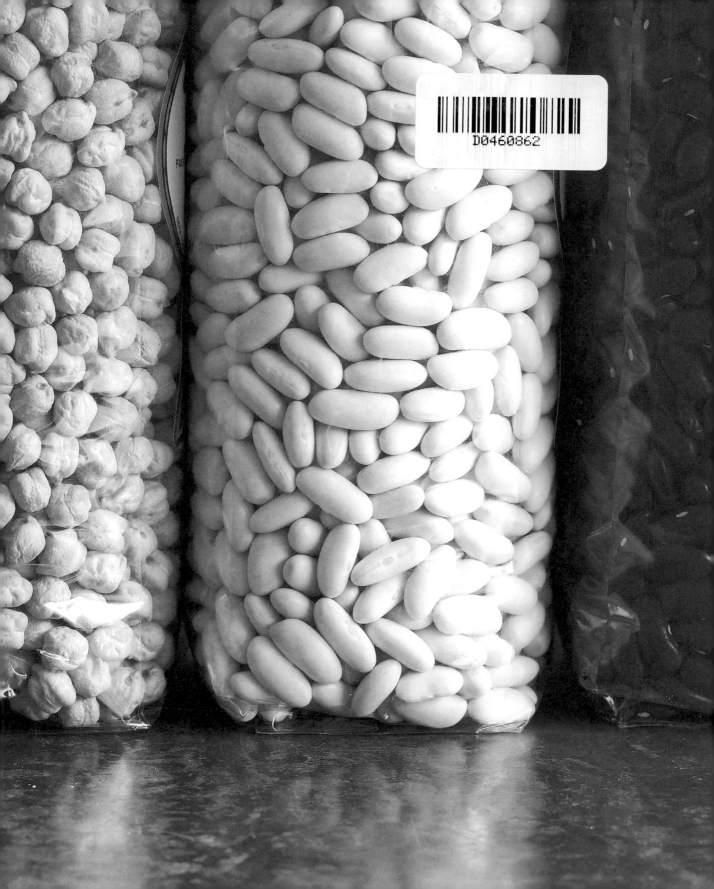

cooking with
wholefoods

cooking with
wholefoods

**healthy and wholesome recipes for
grains, pulses, legumes and beans**

Ross Dobson

photography by Peter Cassidy

LONDON NEW YORK

Dedication

To Mum and Dad. For being my most loyal customers.
It wouldn't be Saturday without you at the café.

Design & Photographic Art Direction Steve Painter
Editor Rebecca Woods
Production Gary Hayes
Editorial Director Julia Charles
Art Director Leslie Harrington

Food Stylist Lizzie Harris
Prop Stylist Róisín Nield
Indexer Vanessa Bird

Author's Acknowledgments

Thanks again to all the crew at Ryland Peters & Small
for the opportunity to work on another wonderful project.
I really missed being in the UK this year but cherished
this opportunity.

First published in 2010
This edition published in 2012 by
Ryland Peters & Small
20–21 Jockey's Fields
London WC1R 4BW
and
519 Broadway, 5th Floor
New York, NY 10012

www.rylandpeters.com

10 9 8 7 6 5 4 3 2 1

Text © Ross Dobson 2010, 2012
Design & photographs © Ryland Peters
& Small 2010, 2012

ISBN: 978-1-84975-334-0

A catalogue record for this book is available from
the British Library.

Library of Congress Cataloging-in-Publication Data
This book was previously cataloged as follows:

Dobson, Ross, 1965-

  Wholesome kitchen : delicious recipes beans, lentils,
grains, and other natural foods / Ross Dobson ;
photography by Peter Cassidy.
    p. cm.
  Includes index.
  ISBN 978-1-84975-035-6
  1. Cookery (Natural foods) I. Title.
  TX741.D623 2010
  641.5'636--dc22

                        2010017909

Printed & bound in China.

Notes

• All spoon measurements are level unless otherwise
specified.

• Eggs are medium unless otherwise specified.
Uncooked or partially cooked eggs should not be
served to the very old, frail, young children, pregnant
women or those with compromised immune systems.

• When a recipe calls for the zest of lemons or limes,
buy unwaxed fruit and wash well before using. If you
can only find treated fruit, scrub well in warm, soapy
water before using.

• Ovens should be preheated to the specified
temperature. Recipes in this book were tested using
a regular oven. If using a fan-assisted oven, follow the
manufacturer's instructions for adjusting temperatures.

7 INTRODUCTION
10 STARTERS
30 SOUPS
52 SALADS
78 SIDES
96 MAIN DISHES
126 SWEET THINGS & BAKING
159 INDEX

CONTENTS

the world's healthiest foods

Beans, lentils, peas and grains have been the most important staple foods in just about every corner of the globe since man first grew and harvested crops. They are nutritious and delicious and can be cooked in hundreds of different and exciting ways to create healthy, satisfying meals. In recent years, more and more interesting and unusual varieties have become available and these make a great addition to any modern cook's repertoire, mine included! Also, as our desire to try new flavours and embrace ideas from cultures other than our own grows, we learn more about the incredible range of ways in which these foods can be prepared and enjoyed.

The recipes in this book have been culled from different styles of cooking from around the world and all feature beans, lentils, peas or grains as their main ingredient (or sometimes a combination of more than one). From simple dips and soups to exotic curries and richly-flavoured casseroles, many of these dishes have ancient roots and there aren't many foods prepared today that have been eaten for thousands of years. For example, Ful Medames (page 13), a simple broad/fava bean dish, was eaten by the pharaohs in Ancient Egypt and is still eaten on the streets of Cairo today.

Pulses are the edible seeds from plants belonging to the legume family, and include chickpeas and a vast array of colourful and tasty beans, from cannellini to pinto. Simple to prepare and sustaining, they have been enjoyed for millennia, by kings and peasants alike. As a convenience food they tick plenty of boxes. Once dried they have a very long shelf life and water is all that's required to cook them. They are also 'wholefoods' in the sense that they have not been tampered with before they reach your plate. They are processed or refined as little as possible, if at all. Even canned or frozen beans contain little, if any, of the bad things such as excessive salt, unhealthy fats or artificial additives and colourings usually found in many 'convenience' foods. The versatility of pulses is best demonstrated by the chickpea and the way it is used to such great effect in Middle Eastern dishes. The hugely popular Lebanese dish of houmous (page 17) is simply a purée of chickpeas with lemon juice, garlic, tahini (sesame seed paste) and olive oil. The addition of these simple ingredients transforms this unassuming little legume into a delicious food stuff that can be enjoyed as a dip, a spread or a sauce. They are also the main ingredient in Falafel (page 22), also a familiar snack often served alongside houmous.

Lentils and dried peas are eaten in India more than anywhere else and are referred to as the 'vegetarian's meat'. Combined with fresh seasonings, such as garlic, ginger and chilli, they make incredible curries, such as the Prawn and Split Yellow Pea Curry (page 116). Although they originated in Asia and North Africa and are still grown there, they are also cultivated in France and Italy. In contrast to the humble dishes of India, the French Puy lentil is highly prized and considered a gourmet ingredient by many. Its nutty bite works well in salads such as the Lentil and Artichoke Salad with Salsa Verde (page 71).

Grains such as wheat, rice, oats, barley and corn have been cultivated throughout the world for centuries. They still form a hugely important part of our diet today and come in many guises from whole grains to finely milled flours. They are used in bread and pasta, baked into cakes or biscuits, or eaten in a less processed form, as a salad ingredient or breakfast cereal. Why not try one of the new ideas I've included here, such as Barley Risotto with Mushrooms and Goat's Cheese (page 120) or Quinoa Choc Chip Cookies (page 131).

I hope you enjoy these recipes and use them to create healthy and balanced meals. Don't be afraid to experiment and create your own favourites too!

STARTERS

carrot and lentil dip

2 carrots, roughly chopped

1 red onion, chopped

1 garlic clove, chopped

1 teaspoon ground cumin

½ teaspoon ground coriander

½ teaspoon sea salt

3 tablespoons olive oil

120 g/½ cup dried red lentils

a handful of fresh coriander/cilantro leaves, finely chopped

Serves 6–8

Preheat the oven to 180°C (350°F) Gas 4. Put the carrots, onion, garlic, cumin, ground coriander, salt and 2 tablespoons of the oil in a bowl. Toss and scatter the vegetables on a baking sheet. Cover with foil and cook in the preheated oven for 45 minutes, until the carrots are just tender. Increase the oven temperature to 220°C (425°F) Gas 7 and cook for a further 10 minutes, until the carrots are golden. Let cool for 10 minutes. Transfer to a food processor and process until chunky. Leave the mixture in the food processor.

Cook the lentils in boiling water for 5 minutes, until just tender. Let sit in the water for 10 minutes then drain well. Add the lentils to the carrot mixture and process until well combined. Transfer to a serving bowl and stir in the remaining oil and the fresh coriander/cilantro. Serve with warmed flat breads.

Moroccan bean and cumin dip

Here is a simple yet tasty dip that is perfect served with toasted flat breads as part of a sharing plate.

300 g/2 cups fresh or frozen broad/fava beans

2 garlic cloves, roughly chopped

½ teaspoon ground cumin

2 tablespoons freshly squeezed lemon juice

65 ml/¼ cup olive oil

1 tablespoon chopped fresh flat leaf parsley leaves

Serves 2–4

Bring a large saucepan of lightly salted water to the boil. Add the broad/fava beans and cook for 5 minutes, until tender. Refresh under cold water and drain well.

Peel the beans, discard the tough skins and put the beans in a food processor with the garlic, cumin and lemon juice and process until well combined but slightly chunky. Season well with salt and stir in the oil. Transfer to a serving bowl and sprinkle with the parsley. Serve with warmed flat breads.

ful medames

This dish is a popular Egyptian breakfast, served with warmed flat bread, sometimes with sliced boiled egg on the side. It is said that the name of the dish, when translated, means to 'bury beans' and comes from a time when the beans were cooked in earthenware pots buried in hot coals.

300 g/1⅓ cups dried broad/fava beans (or canned Egyptian brown beans) with skins removed

250 g/1 cup dried red lentils

2 teaspoons ground cumin

2 tablespoons freshly squeezed lemon juice

65 ml/¼ cup olive oil

1 teaspoon sea salt

Serves 6–8

Rinse the broad/fava beans. Cover with water and soak for at least six hours or overnight. Rinse the beans and drain well then put them in a large saucepan with the lentils and 750 ml/3 cups cold water. Bring to the boil, reduce the heat to low and cover. Cook for 4 hours, barely simmering, until the beans are very soft, thick and mushy. Remove from the heat and stir in the cumin, lemon juice, olive oil and salt. Serve with warmed flat breads.

chunky cannellini bean and tuna dip

This recipe uses a little trick of boiling prepared canned beans for a short while to make them a little more tender before they go in the food processor. You can also do this to soften canned chickpeas before blending them to make houmous.

400-g/14-oz. can cannellini beans, drained
85-g/3-oz. can tuna in olive oil
1 tablespoon olive oil
1 tablespoon small salted capers, well rinsed
1 anchovy fillet (optional)
1 garlic clove, crushed
2 tablespoons chopped fresh flat leaf parsley
sea salt and freshly ground black pepper

Serves 4–6

Put the cannellini beans in a saucepan of boiling water and cook for 1 minute, just to warm through. Drain well, reserving 2 tablespoons of the cooking water. Put the beans, reserved water, tuna, olive oil, capers, anchovy (if using) and garlic in a food processor and process until chunky.

Stir in the parsley and season to taste with salt and pepper. Transfer to a serving bowl and serve with slices of crusty baguette.

spicy chilli bean dip

Shiny, black kidney-shaped black beans are popular in Latin American cooking. They are left whole in this recipe but you could roughly mash after cooking to make them more gooey.

440 g/2 cups dried black beans
2 tablespoons olive oil
1 red onion, chopped
4 garlic cloves, chopped
1 red (bell) pepper, deseeded and diced
1 tablespoon ground cumin
2 teaspoons dried Greek oregano
2 teaspoons chilli powder
2 x 400-g/14-oz. cans chopped tomatoes
a handful of fresh coriander/cilantro leaves, chopped
plain Greek-style yogurt, to serve
warmed corn chips, to serve

Serves 6–8

Put the dried beans in a saucepan with 2 litres/quarts cold water. Bring to the boil, then reduce the heat to a low simmer and cook the beans, uncovered, for about 1½ hours, until just tender and not falling apart. Drain well and set aside.

Heat the oil in a large, heavy-based saucepan set over medium heat. When the oil is hot, add the onion, garlic and pepper and cook for 8–10 minutes, until softened. Stir in the cumin, oregano and chilli powder and fry for 1 minute, until the spices are aromatic.

Increase the heat to high. Add the tomatoes, beans and 250 ml/1 cup cold water and bring to the boil. Reduce the heat to low, partially cover the pan and cook for 1½–2 hours, adding a little more water from time to time if the mixture is drying or catching on the bottom of the pan. Transfer to a serving bowl and serve with the yogurt and coriander/cilantro on top and corn chips for dipping.

houmous

There are as many variations on spelling this as the day is long. And like any other words translated from Arabic to English, its spelling is inconsistent. In Arabic the word simply means 'chickpea' and this ubiquitous dip is more specifically called 'hoummus bi tahina' as it is traditionally made with the addition of tahini sesame paste. While there may be many variations on the name, one thing is for sure, this dip is an essential dish at the meze table with tabbouleh, kibbeh and falafel.

classic:

220 g/1 cup dried chickpeas

3 tablespoons tahini

2 garlic cloves

2 tablespoons freshly squeezed lemon juice

4 tablespoons olive oil

1 teaspoon ground cumin

paprika, to sprinkle

smoky paprika:

1 tablespoon Spanish smoked sweet paprika (pimentón dulce)

3 tablespoons tahini

2 garlic cloves, chopped

2 tablespoons freshly squeezed lemon juice

4 tablespoons olive oil

1½ teaspoons sea salt

lemon and coriander/cilantro:

3 tablespoons tahini

2 garlic cloves, chopped

2 tablespoons freshly squeezed lemon juice

a small handful of fresh coriander/cilantro leaves

4 tablespoons olive oil

1½ teaspoons sea salt

Serves 4–6

Put the chickpeas in a bowl with 1 litre/4 cups cold water and soak for 6 hours or overnight. Bring a large saucepan of water to the boil. Drain the chickpeas and add to the boiling water. Bring to the boil then reduce the heat to a simmer. Cook, uncovered, for about 1 hour, until very tender. Drain over a bowl, reserving the cooking liquid.

For the Classic Houmous, put the chickpeas and 200 ml/¾ cup of the hot cooking liquid in a food processor with the tahini, garlic, lemon juice and cumin and process until smooth. With the motor running, add 3 tablespoons of the oil until smooth and thick. Transfer to a serving plate, making a well in the centre. Pour the remaining oil into the well and sprinkle over the paprika.

For the Smoky Paprika Houmous, soak and cook the chickpeas as above. Transfer to a food processor with 200 ml/¾ cup of the reserved cooking liquid, paprika, tahini, garlic, lemon juice, oil and salt and process to a smooth and thick paste.

For the Lemon and Coriander/Cilantro Houmous, soak and cook the chickpeas as above. Transfer to a food processor with 200 ml/¾ cup of the reserved cooking liquid, tahini, garlic, lemon juice, coriander/cilantro, oil and salt. Process to a smooth and thick paste.

Transfer to a serving bowl or spread out on a large serving plate with toasted flat breads on the side.

chickpea pakoras with mango yogurt

400-g/14-oz. can chickpeas, drained
1 medium potato, chopped
150 g/1 cup frozen peas
65 ml/¼ cup light olive oil
2 large fresh green chillies, finely chopped
2 spring onions/scallions, finely chopped
1 teaspoon finely grated fresh ginger
1 teaspoon each of ground turmeric and cumin
a handful of fresh coriander/cilantro leaves, finely chopped
3 tablespoons besan (chickpea flour)
1 tablespoon freshly squeezed lemon juice
a generous pinch of sea salt

mango yogurt:
3 tablespoons smooth mango chutney
200 ml/¾ cup thick plain yogurt

Makes 24

Cook the chickpeas and potato in a large saucepan of boiling water for 15 minutes, until the potato is tender. Drain well and transfer to a food processor. Process until roughly chopped and chunky. Transfer to a bowl and stir in the peas.

Heat 1 tablespoon of the oil in a frying pan set over medium heat. Add the chillies, spring onions/scallions and ginger and cook for 2–3 minutes, until softened. Stir in the turmeric and cumin and cook for 1 minute, until aromatic. Add this mixture to the chickpea mixture, along with the coriander/cilantro, besan, lemon juice and salt. Stir to just combine. Use your hands to form the mixture into 24 walnut-sized balls, then gently press to flatten each into a pattie.

Heat the remaining oil in a frying pan set over medium/high heat. Cook the patties in batches until golden on both sides. Transfer to a plate lined with paper towels. Swirl the mango chutney into the yogurt and serve alongside the patties.

spiced chickpea and pumpkin fritters

1 tablespoon vegetable oil
1 small red onion, chopped
1 large fresh green chilli, thinly sliced
1 garlic clove, finely chopped
1 teaspoon finely grated fresh ginger
1 teaspoon turmeric
1 teaspoon cumin seeds
1 teaspoon garam masala
500 g/1 lb. peeled pumpkin, cut into large pieces
200 g/1 cup canned chickpeas, well drained and rinsed
40 g/⅓ cup fresh or frozen peas
2 tablespoons besan (chickpea flour)
a handful of fresh coriander/cilantro leaves, roughly chopped
½ teaspoon sea salt
vegetable oil, for deep frying
hot chilli dipping sauce, to serve (optional)

Makes 24

Heat the oil in a frying pan set over high heat and cook the onion, chilli, garlic and ginger for 2–3 minutes, until softened. Stir in the turmeric, cumin and garam masala and cook for 1 minute, until aromatic. Remove from the heat.

Cook the pumpkin in a large saucepan of boiling water for 10 minutes. Add the chickpeas and peas and cook for a further 2 minutes, until the pumpkin is tender. Drain well and roughly mash with a potato masher, making sure the chickpeas are roughly broken up. Combine in a bowl with the onion mixture, besan, coriander/cilantro and salt.

Fill a heavy-based saucepan one-third full with the frying oil and heat over medium/high heat. The oil is ready when surface of the oil is shimmering. Using slightly wet hands, form the mixture into walnut-sized balls and drop them directly into the hot oil, 5–6 at a time, and cook until golden. Transfer to a plate lined with paper towels. Serve with hot chilli sauce for dipping, if liked.

dolmades with green lentils, currants and herbs

Have you ever tried making, and then eating, your own dolmades? These are vine leaves wrapped around a mixture of rice, herbs and sometimes nuts. Good home-made ones bear little or no resemblance to the canned version, which lack freshness and flavour. This recipe has the addition of lentils as well as rice, sweet currants, pine nuts and earthy herbs.

200-g/7-oz. jar vine/grape leaves

1 tablespoon olive oil

1 small onion, finely chopped

165 g/⅔ cup short grain (pudding) rice

45 g/¼ cup dried green lentils

125 ml/½ cup chicken or vegetable stock

2 tablespoons currants

50 g/⅓ cup lightly toasted pine nuts

2 tablespoons finely chopped fresh mint

2 tablespoons finely chopped fresh flat leaf parsley

2 tablespoons finely chopped fresh dill

65 ml/¼ cup extra virgin olive oil

2 tablespoons freshly squeezed lemon juice

sea salt and freshly ground black pepper

Makes 24

To prepare the vine/grape leaves, separate the leaves and soak in cold water for about 15 minutes. Drain well and pat dry with paper towels.

Heat the 1 tablespoon oil in a small saucepan set over high heat and cook the onion for 2–3 minutes, until softened. Stir in the rice and lentils for 1 minute. Add the stock, stir to combine and to remove any grains stuck to the bottom of the pan. Cover and cook over low heat for 10 minutes. Tip the mixture into a bowl and stir in the currants, pine nuts, mint, parsley and dill and season well.

Pick out 24 of the largest, least torn vine leaves to use for the dolmades. Use the remaining leaves to line the base of a large, heavy-based saucepan and pour over half of the extra virgin olive oil.

Lay a vine/grape leaf, vein-side down, on a work surface. Put 1 tablespoon of the filling in the centre of the leaf and fold the stalk end over, bringing the sides in as you roll to enclose the filling. Do not roll up too firmly, as the rice will expand and cause the leaves to split. Repeat to use all the filling. Pack the dolmades into the saucepan, so they fit snugly in one layer. Pour over the remaining oil, lemon juice and 500 ml/2 cups cold water. Gently bring to the boil then reduce heat to low simmer. Cover with an inverted plate and cook over low heat for 45 minutes. Remove from the heat and let sit in the pan for a few minutes and when cool enough to handle, remove from the pan and serve.

falafel with minted yogurt

Many recipes using pulses are Middle Eastern in origin, such as falafel, a popular street food. It is a pattie made using dried chickpeas or broad/fava beans or a combination of the two. This recipe does not cook the beans – they are soaked then puréed before being combined with the other ingredients.

150 g/¾ cup dried broad/fava beans, preferably peeled
220 g/1 cup dried chickpeas
1 large onion, chopped
8 garlic cloves, chopped
a small bunch of fresh flat leaf parsley, chopped
leaves from a bunch of fresh coriander/cilantro, chopped
1 tablespoon ground cumin
2 teaspoons ground coriander
¼ teaspoon chilli powder
2 teaspoons sea salt
vegetable oil, for shallow frying
flat breads, to serve

minted yogurt:
250 ml/1 cup Greek-style yogurt
2 garlic cloves, crushed
a handful of fresh mint leaves, finely chopped

Makes about 30

Soak the broad/fava beans in cold water for 24 hours. Soak the chickpeas in cold water for at least 12 hours or overnight. If using unpeeled broad/fava beans you will need to rub the skins off and discard them.

Put the broad/fava beans in a food processor and process until fine and crumbly. Transfer to a large bowl. Do the same with the chickpeas, putting them in the bowl with the broad/fava beans.

Put the onion, garlic, parsley and fresh coriander/cilantro in a food processor and process until well combined. Add this mixture to the beans with the cumin, ground coriander, chilli powder and salt. Use a large spoon to combine the mixture. Set aside and let sit for 30 minutes.

Put sufficient oil in a frying pan to come about 2.5 cm/1 inch up the side and heat over low/medium heat. The oil is ready when the surface is shimmering and a pinch of the mixture sizzles on contact with the oil.

Using two dessertspoons, form the mixture into oval patties. Drop directly into the hot oil and cook for 2–3 minutes, turning halfway through until golden and crispy. Transfer to a plate lined with paper towels.

To make the minted yogurt, put the yogurt, garlic and mint in a bowl and stir well to combine.

Serve the falafel wrapped in flat breads and dressed with the minted yogurt.

salt cod, potato and butter bean fritters

Salt cod (bacalao) is a very full-flavoured ingredient and one of the most popular foods of Spain and Portugal. Potatoes make the perfect partner to the cod in these light and crispy fritters and are the traditional ingredient but the addition of butter beans makes them smoother and creamier. Serve with plenty of lemon wedges for squeezing and a little aioli, if liked.

400 g/14 oz. salt cod

200 g/7 oz. floury potatoes, quartered

50 g/⅓ cup canned butter beans, drained and well rinsed

2 tablespoons milk

2 tablespoons olive oil

2 garlic cloves, crushed

30 g/3½ tablespoons plain/all-purpose flour

¼ teaspoon baking powder

2 eggs, separated

2 spring onions/scallions, finely chopped

a small handful of fresh flat leaf parsley leaves, finely chopped

light olive oil, for frying

lemon wedges, to serve

Makes about 36

Soak the salt cod in cold water for 24 hours, changing the water every 6 hours.

Cook the potatoes in boiling water for 15 minutes, until tender. Add the beans and cook for 5 minutes. Drain well and put into a bowl. Mash with the milk and oil until chunky and well combined.

Drain the cod and cut into large chunks. Put into a saucepan and add sufficient water to fully submerge the cod. Bring to the boil and cook for 10–15 minutes, until the water surface is frothy and the fish is tender. Drain and let cool for a few minutes. When cool enough to handle, pick out any bones and flake the flesh with a fork.

Add the cod to the potatoes with the garlic, flour, baking powder, egg yolks, spring onions/scallions and parsley. Whisk the egg whites until peaking then fold into the potato mixture until combined.

Fill a large heavy-based saucepan one-third full with oil and heat over medium/high heat. The oil is ready when the surface is shimmering and a pinch of the fritter mixture sizzles on contact.

Drop heaped tablespoons of the fritter mixture into the hot oil, without overcrowding the pan, and cook for about 2 minutes, until golden and puffed. Transfer to a plate lined with paper towels.

chicken, white bean and herb terrine

Summer or winter, a terrine makes a fabulous starter or lunch dish. White beans are combined with chicken thigh, which in my opinion is much tastier than the breast. This can be made a day or two in advance and in fact benefits from this as flavours develop. Any tangy, chilli-spiked chutney or relish will do but fruity mango chutney adds another level of interest.

500 g/1 lb. skinless chicken thigh fillet, cut into bite-sized pieces

a handful of fresh flat leaf parsley leaves, finely chopped

1 teaspoon fresh thyme leaves

2 garlic cloves, chopped

1 teaspoon finely grated orange zest

3 tablespoons brandy

½ teaspoon sea salt

½ teaspoon sugar

400-g/14-oz. can cannellini beans, drained and well rinsed

1 egg, beaten

12 rashers lean back bacon

to serve:

mango chutney

toasted bread

a simple green salad

a medium non-stick loaf pan

a large roasting pan, big enough to take the loaf pan

Serves 6–8

Combine the chicken, parsley, thyme, garlic, orange zest, brandy, salt and sugar in a bowl. Cover and refrigerate overnight, stirring occasionally.

Preheat the oven to 180°C (350°F) Gas 4.

Remove the chicken mixture from the refrigerator and stir in the cannellini beans and beaten egg until well combined.

Lay the bacon rashers down the length of the loaf pan, making sure they overlap slightly and hang over the sides. Put the chicken mixture in the pan, firmly pressing down into the pan. Fold the overhanging bacon rashers over to enclose the mixture in the pan and cover firmly with a layer of foil, pressing firmly around the edge to seal.

Sit the loaf pan in the larger roasting pan and add enough water to come halfway up the sides of the pan. Cook in the preheated oven for 1½ hours. Allow the terrine to cool in the pan, covered.

Thickly slice and serve with mango chutney, toasted bread and a simple green salad.

black lentils with lemon juice

This popular lentil dish can be found all over the Middle East from Lebanon to Iraq. Use Indian black lentils (urad daal) if you can find them – they are nutty with a chewy texture and very similar to French Puy lentils. You'll find them in Indian grocers or health food stores. If you can't find them substitute Puy. Serve with strips of warmed pitta bread for dipping.

450 g/2 cups black lentils

2 medium potatoes, roughly chopped

2 tablespoons plain/all-purpose flour

3 tablespoons olive oil

4 garlic cloves, chopped

2 shallots, thinly sliced

a small bunch of fresh coriander/cilantro, finely chopped

65 ml/¼ cup freshly squeezed lemon juice

sea salt and freshly ground black pepper

pitta bread, to serve

Serves 4–6

Put the lentils in a saucepan with 750 ml/3 cups cold water. Set over high heat, bring to the boil and cook for 15 minutes. Add the potatoes and cook for a further 15 minutes, until the lentils and potatoes are just tender.

Combine the flour and 2–3 tablespoons cold water in a small bowl to make a smooth paste. Add to the lentils, stirring well to combine and cook for 2 minutes, until the lentil mixture has thickened. Remove from the heat.

Heat the oil in a frying pan set over medium heat. Add the garlic and shallots, cook for 1 minute, then add to the lentils along with the coriander/cilantro and lemon juice. Season well and serve warm or cold.

lamb kibbeh with garlic sauce

Here, softened bulgur wheat is moulded around a lamb mixture to make sausage shapes. This is a Syrian recipe, as is the pungent sauce. The strong garlic flavour will linger on the palate for hours after eating – in a good way!

235 g/1½ cups fine bulgur wheat

125 g/4 oz. lean lamb mince

1 onion, grated

½ teaspoon allspice

½ teaspoon ground cumin

filling:

1 tablespoon olive oil

1 small onion, finely chopped

2 garlic cloves, chopped

100 g/3 oz. lean lamb mince

¼ teaspoon allspice

¼ teaspoon ground cinnamon

2 tablespoons pine nuts, lightly toasted and roughly chopped

a large handful of fresh mint leaves, finely chopped

sea salt and freshly ground black pepper

vegetable oil, for frying

garlic sauce:

6 garlic cloves, peeled

¼ teaspoon sea salt

175 ml/¾ cup real/whole-egg mayonnaise

a baking sheet, lined with baking paper

Serves 4–6

Put the bulgur in a small heatproof bowl. Pour over enough boiling water to completely cover and leave for 5 minutes. Tip the bulgur into a fine sieve/strainer and press down to remove as much water as possible. Leave to drain.

Put the bulgur, lamb, onion, allspice and cumin in a food processor and process to a paste, scraping down the sides of the bowl from time to time. Transfer to a bowl, cover and refrigerate for at least 1 hour.

For the filling, heat the oil in a frying pan set over high heat. Add the onion and garlic and stir-fry for 4–5 minutes, until softened and golden, Add the lamb, allspice and cinnamon and stir-fry for 4–5 minutes, until the lamb is brown and aromatic. Transfer to a bowl and stir in the pine nuts and mint. Season well and let cool.

Take about 2 tablespoons of the bulgur mixture and roll in slightly wet hands to form an oval, log shape about 6 cm/ 2½ inches long. With wet hands, use your thumb to press an indentation down the centre of the log. Fill this with about 2 teaspoons of the lamb filling. Mould around the bulgur mixture to enclose, forming a torpedo shape. Repeat to make 15 in total and put on the prepared baking sheet. Refrigerate for at least 1 hour.

Pour in sufficient oil to come one-third of the way up the side of a large frying pan. Set over medium heat. The oil is ready when the surface is shimmering and a pinch of the mixture sizzles on contact. Add several kibbeh at a time and cook for 2–3 minutes, turning often so they cook to an even golden colour all over. Transfer to a plate lined with paper towels.

To make the sauce, chop the garlic and sprinkle the salt over the top. Continue chopping until the garlic forms a paste. Put in a bowl with the mayonnaise and stir well to combine. Serve alongside the kibbeh.

SOUPS

three sisters soup

Referred to as 'the three sisters' by native American Indians, beans, corn and squash are an indelible part of this cuisine.

50 g/¼ cup dried butter beans

4 ripe Italian plum tomatoes
(such as Roma)

1 large fresh jalapeño chilli

4 garlic cloves, unpeeled

2 tablespoons olive oil

1 onion, chopped

2 cobs/ears of fresh (sweet)corn,
shucked

100 g/4 oz. small yellow squash
(pattypan or similar), quartered

100 g/4 oz. fine green beans,
trimmed and halved

500 ml/2 cups vegetable stock

2 tablespoons freshly squeezed
lime juice

a handful of fresh coriander/cilantro
sprigs, roughly chopped

sea salt

Serves 4

Soak the butter beans in cold water overnight. Drain and put in a large saucepan with sufficient cold water to cover. Bring to the boil, reduce the heat and simmer, uncovered, for 1 hour, until tender. Drain and set aside.

Preheat the oven to 220°C (425°F) Gas 7.

Put the tomatoes, chilli and garlic on a baking sheet and cook in the preheated oven for about 10–15 minutes, until the skins darken and begin to blister. Remove the baking sheet from the oven, transfer everything to a clean plastic bag and seal. When cool enough to handle, peel the tomatoes, chilli and garlic. Discard the skins, and coarsely chop the flesh. Set aside.

Heat the oil in a large saucepan set over medium heat. Add the onion and (sweet)corn with a pinch of salt and cook for 10 minutes, stirring often until softened. Stir in the tomato mixture, squash, green beans, butter beans and stock and bring to the boil. Reduce the heat to medium and simmer, uncovered, for 10 minutes, until the green beans are tender. Stir in the lime juice, garnish with a few small sprigs of coriander/cilantro and serve.

creamy curried parsnip and butter bean soup

This is a real winter warmer, perfect for a weekend dinner at the end of a cold day. Don't overlook the parsnip, it's a really tasty root veggie and inexpensive too at the right time of year, just when you want to eat it most.

2 tablespoons butter

1 onion, chopped

2 garlic cloves, chopped

2 tablespoons mild curry powder

500 g/1 lb. parsnips, chopped

1 litre/4 cups vegetable stock

400-g/14-oz. can butter beans, well drained and rinsed

125 ml/½ cup single/light cream

1–2 tablespoons freshly snipped chives

sea salt and freshly ground black pepper

warmed flat breads, to serve

Serves 4

Heat the butter in a large saucepan set over medium heat. When the butter is sizzling, add the onion and garlic with a pinch of salt and cook for 10 minutes, until the onion is soft.

Stir in the curry powder and cook for 1 minute until aromatic. Add the parsnips, stock and beans and bring to the boil. Reduce the heat and simmer, uncovered, for 30 minutes, until the parsnips and beans are tender.

Remove from the heat and let cool for about 10 minutes. Transfer the mixture in batches to a food processor and process until smooth. Return the soup to a clean saucepan and set over low heat. Stir in the cream and season to taste with salt and pepper. Sprinkle over the chives. Serve with warmed flat breads.

pasta e fagioli

This hearty soup of pasta and beans is a classic from the Puglia region of Italy. In my version of the recipe I like to replace the beans with creamy chickpeas and, if liked, you can add some diced chorizo or pancetta to the pan when you cook off the onions. The pasta shapes traditionally used are orecchiette, meaning 'little ears' but any small shape will work just as well.

250 g/1¼ cups dried chickpeas
2 tablespoons olive oil
1 onion, finely chopped
2 garlic cloves, finely chopped
a sprig of fresh rosemary
¼ teaspoon dried chilli/hot
pepper flakes
400-g/14-oz can chopped tomatoes
1 tablespoon tomato purée/paste
1.5 litres/6 cups vegetable stock
100 g/⅔ cup small pasta shapes such
as orecchiette or conchigliette
sea salt and freshly ground
black pepper

to serve:
freshly grated Parmesan
extra virgin olive oil

Serves 4

Soak the chickpeas in cold water overnight. Drain and put in a large saucepan with sufficient cold water to cover. Bring to the boil, reduce the heat to medium and cook, uncovered, for 45 minutes, until very tender. Drain and set aside.

Heat the oil in a large, heavy-based saucepan set over medium heat. Add the onion, garlic, rosemary and chilli/hot pepper flakes along with a pinch of salt and cook for 8–10 minutes, stirring often, until the onion has softened.

Increase the heat to high. Stir in the tomatoes, tomato purée/paste, stock and the chickpeas and bring to the boil. Add the pasta, reduce the heat to a medium simmer and cook for about 20 minutes, until the pasta is tender. Season to taste with salt and pepper.

Serve sprinkled with Parmesan and drizzled with olive oil.

Moroccan harira

Variations of this soup can be found throughout the Islamic world. In Morocco there are at least a dozen versions but most include lamb, chickpeas, lentils and spicy cumin. Thick and hearty, this recipe is somewhere between a soup and a stew and can be served as a meal on its own with plenty of crusty bread for dunking. Also, I really don't like using too many pots and pans so this is all done in one large saucepan.

2 tablespoons butter

2 tablespoons olive oil

2 onions, chopped

3 garlic cloves, chopped

2 teaspoons ground cumin

2 teaspoons paprika

1 bay leaf

1 litre/4 cups beef stock

2 tablespoons tomato purée/paste

400-g/14-oz. can chopped tomatoes

500 g/1 lb. lamb shoulder meat, cut into bite-sized pieces

410-g/14-oz. can chickpeas, drained and well rinsed

50 g/¼ cup dried brown lentils

leaves from a small bunch of fresh coriander/cilantro, roughly chopped

sea salt and freshly ground black pepper

lemon wedges, to serve

Serves 4

Heat the butter and oil in a large, heavy-based saucepan set over medium heat. When the butter is sizzling, add the onion and garlic along with a pinch of salt and cook for 8–10 minutes, stirring often until softened.

Stir in the cumin, paprika and bay leaf and cook for 1 minute, until aromatic. Add the stock, tomato purée/paste, tomatoes and lamb pieces and bring to the boil. Reduce the heat to a low simmer, partially cover and cook for 1 hour. Add the chickpeas and lentils and cook for 1 hour more, until the lamb is very tender and the lentils cooked through. Season to taste with salt and pepper and sprinkle over the coriander/cilantro. Serve with the lemon wedges on the side to squeeze into the soup and crusty bread.

Vegetarian option: Reduce the stock quantity by half (and use vegetable stock). Instead of adding the lamb to the pan with the stock, tomato purée/paste and tomatoes, add the chickpeas and lentils and let it all gently simmer over low heat until the lentils have softened and the soup thickened.

smoky chorizo and bean soup

Here's a short and simple recipe. Small bowls of this can be served up as part of a tapas-style buffet, served with garlicky toasted baguette slices on the side.

2 tablespoons olive oil
200 g/7 oz. chorizo sausage
1 red onion, thinly sliced
2 garlic cloves, chopped
¼ teaspoon Spanish smoked sweet paprika (pimentón dulce)
400-g/14-oz. can chopped tomatoes
500 ml/2 cups chicken or vegetable stock
410-g/14-oz. can haricot/navy beans, drained and well rinsed
a handful each of fresh flat leaf parsley and fresh coriander/cilantro leaves, roughly chopped
toasted baguette slices, rubbed with garlic, to serve

Serves 4

Heat the oil in a large saucepan set over high heat. Add the chorizo, onion and garlic and cook for 5 minutes, until the chorizo has browned and the onion has softened.

Stir in the paprika for 1 minute, until aromatic. Add the tomatoes, stock and beans and bring to the boil. Reduce the heat to a medium simmer and cook, uncovered, for 10 minutes. Stir in the parsley and coriander/cilantro and serve with garlic toasts.

Vegetarian option: Replace the chorizo with 400 g/2 cups sliced mushrooms and cook as you would the chorizo. Be sure to use vegetable stock and stir through a few handfuls of baby spinach leaves until wilted for some extra flavour.

creamy cannellini, leek and sorrel soup

The sharp, lemon flavour of sorrel is highly prized in France where it is often teamed with dairy and eggs in classic dishes. Here it works nicely with the pleasingly smooth and creamy texture of cannellini beans.

50 g/3 tablespoons butter
1 leek, trimmed and sliced
2 garlic cloves, chopped
100 g/3 slices (streaky) bacon, thinly sliced
2 boiling potatoes (such as desirée), diced
1 litre/4 cups vegetable or chicken stock
410-g/14-oz. can cannellini beans, drained and well rinsed
1 bunch sorrel, thinly sliced
125 ml/½ cup double/heavy cream
a handful of fresh flat leaf parsley leaves, finely chopped
sea salt and freshly ground black pepper

Serves 4

Heat the butter in a large saucepan set over medium heat. When the butter is sizzling, add the leek, garlic and bacon and cook for 10 minutes, until the leek is softened and silky looking and the bacon is golden.

Add the potatoes, stock and beans and bring to the boil. Reduce the heat to a medium simmer and cook for about 20 minutes, until the potatoes are tender. Stir in the sorrel and cook for a further 5 minutes, until the sorrel has wilted. Stir in the cream and season to taste with salt and pepper. Scatter the parsley over the top and serve.

Vegetarian option: Simply omit the bacon and use vegetable stock for a satisfying meat-free soup.

spicy pinto bean soup with shredded lettuce and sour cream

A smaller, paler version of the borlotti bean, the pinto has an attractive orange-pink skin with rust-coloured specks. It's used extensively in Mexican cuisine, most familiarly in frijoles refritos *(refried beans). Earthy and savoury in flavour, the beans go well with tomatoes, peppers and coriander/cilantro – pretty much all the best-loved flavours of the Americas.*

100 g/½ cup dried pinto beans
2 tablespoons butter
1 tablespoon olive oil
1 red onion, chopped
2 garlic cloves, chopped
1 red bell pepper, deseeded and diced
2 carrots, chopped
2 teaspoons chilli powder
2 teaspoons ground cumin
2 bay leaves
1.5 litres/6 cups vegetable stock
400-g/14-oz. can chopped tomatoes
sea salt

to serve:
1 small iceberg lettuce, finely shredded
sour cream
leaves from a small bunch of fresh coriander/cilantro
lime wedges

Serves 4

Soak the beans in cold water overnight. Drain and set aside.

Heat the butter and oil in a large, heavy-based saucepan set over medium heat. Add the onion, garlic, red pepper and carrots along with a pinch of salt. Cook for 10 minutes, until softened. Stir in the chilli powder, cumin and bay leaves and cook for 1 minute, until aromatic.

Increase the heat to high. Add the stock, tomatoes and beans and bring to the boil. Reduce the heat to a medium simmer and cook, uncovered, for about 45 minutes, until the beans are tender.

Serve topped with shredded lettuce, a dollop of sour cream and a few coriander/cilantro leaves. Offer lime wedges on the side for squeezing.

brown lentil and Swiss chard soup

Using fresh, seasonal ingredients simply prepared is the secret of any good recipe, including this one. Sometimes referred to as continental lentils, the hearty disc-shaped pulses used here do not disintegrate when cooked so make an ideal ingredient for rustic soups and casseroles. For a more substantial soup, add diced chicken breast along with the Swiss chard and let it gently poach in the stock, until just cooked through and tender.

1 litre/4 cups vegetable or chicken stock

280 g/1⅓ cups dried brown lentils

65 ml/¼ cup olive oil

1 onion, chopped

4 garlic cloves, finely chopped

850 g/1 lb. 14 oz. Swiss chard, trimmed and thinly sliced

65 ml/¼ cup freshly squeezed lemon juice

leaves from a small bunch of fresh coriander/cilantro, roughly chopped

sea salt and freshly ground black pepper

Serves 4

Put the stock and lentils in a large saucepan set over high heat and bring to the boil. Reduce the heat to medium and cook for 1 hour, uncovered, until the lentils are tender. Reduce the heat to low.

Heat the oil in a large frying pan set over high heat. Add the onion and garlic along with a pinch of salt. Cook for 4–5 minutes, stirring often, until softened.

Stir in the Swiss chard and stir-fry for 2–3 minutes, until wilted. Add the chard mixture to the lentils and cook over low heat for 10 minutes.

Stir in the lemon juice and coriander/cilantro and season to taste with salt and pepper. Serve immediately.

lamb and vegetable soup with split peas and barley

Dried peas come from the field pea not the garden pea, which is eaten fresh. They are available whole or split and the latter have a sweeter flavour which works well here with winter veggies.

125 g/⅔ cup dried split yellow peas
2 onions, chopped
1 celery stick, sliced into crescents
2 carrots, chopped
2 small turnips, chopped
125 g/⅔ cup pearl barley
500 g/1 lb. lamb shoulder meat, cut into bite-sized chunks
leaves from a small bunch of fresh flat leaf parsley, finely chopped
2 litres/quarts chicken or vegetable stock
sea salt and freshly ground black pepper
warmed rye or brown bread rolls, to serve

Serves 4

Soak the spilt peas in cold water for 6 hours. Drain and put in a large saucepan with the onions, celery, carrots, turnips, barley, lamb, half of the parsley and chicken stock.

Bring to the boil, then reduce the heat to a low simmer. Partially cover and cook for 2 hours, stirring frequently, until the lamb, peas and barley are very tender. Season to taste with salt and pepper, sprinkle with the remaining parsley and serve with warmed bread rolls.

Vegetarian option: Turn this recipe into a hearty root vegetable soup by omitting the lamb and adding 1 chopped parsnip, 8 small waxy potatoes and 300 g/ 10 oz. chopped pumpkin flesh. Cook until the veggies are tender.

pea and ham soup

This old school favourite is a homely, no-nonsense recipe packed with moist and richly flavoured ham. I use smoked ham hocks here but the best thing, really, is the leftover hock from a Christmas ham.

2 tablespoons butter

2 onions, finely chopped

1 carrot, roughly chopped

1 celery stick, roughly chopped

300 g/1½ cups dried green split peas

a handful of fresh flat leaf parsley leaves, finely chopped, plus extra to garnish

1 teaspoon fresh thyme leaves

2 smoked ham hocks

2 litres/quarts chicken or vegetable stock

sea salt and freshly ground black pepper

buttered toast, to serve

Serves 4

Heat the butter in a large saucepan set over medium heat. When the butter is sizzling, add the onions, carrot and celery and cook for 10 minutes, stirring often, until the vegetables have softened.

Stir in the peas, parsley and thyme for 1 minute. Add the ham hocks and stock. Increase the heat to high and bring to the boil. Reduce the heat to a low simmer, partially cover and cook for 2 hours, stirring often to prevent the peas from catching on the bottom of the pan.

Remove the pan from the heat and let cool to room temperature. Remove the ham bones and cut off any fat and skin and discard. Remove the meat and shred. Return the shredded meat to the soup. Return the pan to low heat and cook for 10–15 minutes, just to heat through. Season to taste, ladle into bowls and garnish with flat leaf parsley and black pepper. Serve with buttered toast.

fresh shiitake and barley soup

Fresh shiitake add a satisfying texture to this hearty soup but any variety of fresh mushroom could be used. Dried shiitake are inexpensive and have a long shelf life so make a good storecupboard staple.

8 dried shiitake mushrooms
1 tablespoon butter
1 tablespoon vegetable oil
4 spring onions/scallions, thinly sliced
2 garlic cloves, chopped
1 celery stick, chopped
1 carrot, chopped
250 g/9 oz. fresh shiitake mushrooms, chopped
2 litres/quarts vegetable stock
200 g/1 cup pearl or pot barley

Serves 4

Put the dried mushrooms in a heatproof bowl and pour over 1 litre/4 cups boiling water. Let soak for 30 minutes. Reserve 125 ml/½ cup of the soaking liquid. Squeeze out as much liquid as possible from the mushrooms, cut off the stems and discard them. Finely slice the caps and set aside.

Heat the butter and oil in a large saucepan set over medium heat. When the butter is sizzling, add the spring onions/scallions, garlic, celery, carrot and fresh mushrooms. Cook for 10 minutes, stirring often, until softened. Add the stock, barley, reserved soaking liquid and dried mushrooms and bring to the boil. Reduce the heat to a medium simmer and cook for about 40 minutes, until the barley is tender. (Pot barley will require a longer cooking time.) Serve immediately.

barley and autumn vegetable soup

This soup has a definite Asian feel to it, with the addition of tamari and sesame oil. But feel free to hold back on the sesame oil and add a sprinkling of finely grated Parmesan on top. The unami (savoury flavour element of the cheese) complements the tamari.

2 tablespoons butter
1 leek, trimmed and sliced
1 carrot, chopped
250 g/9 oz. peeled pumpkin, chopped
250 g/9 oz. brown mushrooms, sliced
2 medium potatoes, chopped
2 litres/quarts vegetable stock
200 g/1 cup pearl or pot barley
¼ teaspoon ground white pepper
2 tablespoons tamari or dark soy sauce
500 g/1 lb. kale, finely shredded
2 spring onions/scallions, thinly sliced on the angle (optional)
1 teaspoon sesame oil

Serves 4

Heat the butter in a large saucepan set over medium heat. Add the leek and carrot and cook for 10 minutes, stirring often, until the vegetables have softened. Add the pumpkin, mushrooms, potatoes, stock, barley and pepper and bring to the boil. Reduce the heat to a medium simmer and cook for 45–50 minutes, until the barley is tender. (Pot barley will require a longer cooking time.)

Stir in the tamari and kale and cook for 10 minutes, until the kale is wilted. Serve immediately with a sprinkling of spring onions/scallions (if using) and drizzled with sesame oil.

SALADS

bean, feta and dill salad

The season for fresh, young broad/fava beans is short. They need very little preparation; just throw them into some boiling water, rinse, drain and add to whatever you like, from pastas and risottos to salads. Older and frozen broad/fava beans can of course be used but they need a little more attention. As they age, the skins toughen so need to be slipped off after cooking.

500 g/3 cups fresh young broad/fava beans
65 ml/¼ cup olive oil
1 small red onion, finely chopped
2 garlic cloves, finely chopped
a small bunch of fresh dill, finely chopped
a handful of fresh flat leaf parsley leaves
a handful of small fresh mint leaves
2 tablespoons freshly squeezed lemon juice
100 g/4 oz. feta cheese, roughly crumbled
freshly ground black pepper

Serves 4

Cook the broad/fava beans in a large saucepan of boiling water for 10 minutes. Rinse under cold water and drain well. (If using older broad/fava beans, slip the skins off and discard.)

Heat 1 tablespoon of the oil in a small frying pan set over medium heat. Add the onion and garlic and cook for 2–3 minutes, until just softened. Remove from the heat.

Put the broad/fava beans and herbs in a bowl. Whisk together the remaining oil and lemon juice in a small bowl and pour over the salad. Stir to combine. Add the feta, stir again, and season well with black pepper before serving.

pancetta and bean salad

This is a wonderfully full-flavoured salad or side dish. Pancetta is a fatty bacon that is the Italian equivalent of streaky bacon. It is cured by traditional methods and may be unsmoked or smoked – smoked is preferable for this recipe for an extra level of flavour.

8 slices smoked pancetta
1 kg/5 cups fresh young broad/fava beans
sea salt and freshly ground black pepper

dressing:
3 tablespoons olive oil
2 teaspoons red wine vinegar
1 teaspoon Dijon mustard
1 garlic clove, crushed
½ teaspoon fresh thyme leaves

Serves 4

To make the dressing, whisk all the ingredients together in a small bowl and set aside.

Preheat the oven to 180°C (350°F) Gas 4. Lay the pancetta slices on a baking sheet, ensuring they are not overlapping, and cook in the preheated oven for 5 minutes. Turn the pancetta over and cook for another 5 minutes. Remove from the oven and let cool. When cool enough to handle, roughly tear up the pancetta into smaller pieces and set aside.

Bring a large saucepan of water to the boil and cook the broad/fava beans for 10 minutes, until tender. Drain well and transfer to a bowl of iced water to chill. Drain and transfer to a bowl. Pour in the salad dressing and add the pancetta pieces. Season to taste with salt and pepper and gently toss to combine. Serve immediately.

slow-cooked lamb salad with beans, pomegranate and fresh mint

Broad/fava beans, fresh or dried, have fed man for millennia. Using them in this recipe results in my favourite type of food to eat; simple, casual and flavoursome. Preparing lamb shoulder cannot be rushed; when cooked with patience it will melt in your mouth.

2 tablespoons light olive oil

1 tablespoon sea salt

1 tablespoon ground cumin

2 kg/4 lbs. bone-in lamb shoulder

500 g/1 lb. fresh young broad/fava beans

leaves from a bunch of fresh mint

seeds from 1 pomegranate

2 tablespoons extra virgin olive oil

2 tablespoons freshly squeezed lemon juice

sea salt and freshly ground black pepper

a rack set over a baking sheet or roasting pan

Serves 6

Preheat the oven to 160°C (325°F) Gas 3. Rub the light olive oil and then the salt and cumin all over the lamb. Sit the lamb on a rack set over a large baking sheet and cook in the preheated oven for 6 hours. Remove, lightly cover with foil and let rest for up to 3 hours.

Cook the broad/fava beans in a large saucepan of boiling water for 10 minutes, until just tender. Drain well.

Use a fork or your fingers to shred the lamb off of the bone. Transfer to a bowl and add the broad/fava beans, mint leaves, pomegranate seeds, extra virgin olive oil and lemon juice. Toss to combine, season to taste with salt and pepper and serve immediately.

spicy three-bean salad

Growing up in Australia, there was a ubiquitous canned 'three-bean salad', which was supposed to be eaten with the gloopy sauce it came in. Sorry, but no way! Not when you can make your own delicious and wholesome salad like this one. If you don't have the time to soak the beans overnight, simply replace each of the dried weight with a 400-g/14-oz. can of drained and rinsed beans, then toss with the other ingredients.

50 g/¼ cup dried kidney beans

50 g/¼ cup dried cannellini beans

50 g/¼ cup dried broad/fava beans

2 ripe tomatoes

65 ml/¼ cup olive oil

1 fresh green jalapeño chilli, deseeded and thinly sliced

1 small red onion, thinly sliced

2 garlic cloves, finely chopped

1 tablespoon white wine vinegar

leaves from a small bunch of fresh coriander/cilantro, finely chopped

leaves from a small bunch of fresh flat leaf parsley, roughly chopped

sea salt and freshly ground black pepper

crusty bread, to serve

Serves 4

Put all of the beans in a large bowl. Cover with cold water and leave to soak for 12 hours.

Drain the beans and discard the water. Cook the beans in a large saucepan of boiling water for 1 hour, until they are tender. Drain and transfer to a large bowl.

Cut the tomatoes in half. Squeeze out and discard as many of the seeds as possible and roughly chop the flesh. Add to the beans.

Combine the oil, chilli, onion and garlic in a small saucepan and set over medium heat. When the ingredients start to sizzle in the oil, remove from the heat and add to the beans and tomatoes. Stir in the vinegar, season to taste with salt and pepper and stir in the coriander/cilantro and parsley. Serve at room temperature or chilled, as preferred, with plenty of crusty bread.

roast chicken and chickpea salad with olives and capers

This is a wonderfully simple summer lunch recipe – one, in fact, that I cook in my café.

110 g/⅔ cup dried chickpeas

110 g/⅔ cup pitted kalamata olives

40 g/3 tablespoons salted capers, well rinsed, drained and roughly chopped

2 small red onions, thinly sliced

2 garlic cloves, finely chopped

4 salted anchovies, finely chopped (optional)

leaves from a large bunch of fresh flat leaf parsley, finely chopped

65 ml/¼ cup freshly squeezed lemon juice

85 ml/⅓ cup olive oil

1 cooked chicken (rotisserie is ideal)

1 teaspoon Spanish smoked sweet paprika (pimentón dulce)

Serves 4

Put the chickpeas in a bowl and cover with cold water. Let soak for 6 hours or overnight.

Drain the chickpeas well and cook in a large saucepan of boiling water for about 30 minutes, until tender. Rinse under cold water, drain well and transfer to a large bowl. Add the olives, capers, onions, garlic, anchovies (if using), parsley, lemon juice and oil. Stir well to combine.

Remove the meat from the chicken and thinly slice. Add to the bowl with the other ingredients and stir to combine. Sprinkle the paprika over the top and serve immediately.

Vegetarian option: Omit the chicken and anchovies and double the chickpea quantity. Stir in 500 g/16 oz. thinly sliced firm tofu. Let sit at room temperature for about 1 hour, stirring often, so that the tofu is infused with the flavours of the dressing.

heirloom tomato salad with borlotti beans, mozzarella and summer herbs

When it comes to tomatoes, here in my native Australia we are spoilt for choice during the summer months, so I like to choose more than one interesting variety, heirloom if possible. Plenty of garden-fresh herbs make the perfect partner for the smooth borlotti beans and creamy mozzarella, making this a delicious main course salad to enjoy in the warmer months.

100 g/½ cup dried borlotti beans

65 ml/¼ cup extra virgin olive oil

750 g/1½ lbs. mixed heirloom tomatoes

1 teaspoon fine sea salt

250 g/9 oz. fresh mozzarella cheese (buffalo, if available)

a handful of fresh basil leaves, roughly torn

a handful of fresh flat leaf parsley leaves, roughly chopped

a handful of fresh mint leaves, roughly chopped

sea salt and freshly ground black pepper

crusty bread, to serve

Serves 4

Put the beans in a bowl, cover with cold water and let soak overnight.

Drain the beans and cook in a large saucepan of boiling water for 40–45 minutes, until tender but not breaking apart. Rinse under cold water, drain well and put in a bowl. Stir in 1 tablespoon of the olive oil and season well with salt and pepper. Set aside or refrigerate until needed (removing from the refrigerator about 30 minutes before serving).

Thinly slice the larger tomatoes and arrange them on a serving plate. Cut any smaller tomatoes in half and tumble over the tomato slices. Sprinkle sea salt over the tomatoes and set aside for 15 minutes to allow the flavours to develop.

Roughly tear the mozzarella into bite-sized pieces and arrange over the tomatoes. Scatter the herbs over the top and spoon the beans over and around the salad. Drizzle the remaining olive oil over the salad and serve immediately with crusty bread.

Spanish bread salad with chickpeas, chorizo and baby spinach

Hidden in chorizo are spices that can be enticed out and used to flavour the oil it is cooked in. The warm, spiced pan juices are then tossed with the other ingredients so that the heat gently wilts the spinach. Try substituting chorizo with smoked bacon or pancetta and adding a little extra pimentón.

4 thick slices sourdough bread

3 tablespoons olive oil

2 garlic cloves, peeled and left whole

2 chorizo sausages, thinly sliced

1 red onion, thinly sliced

½ teaspoon Spanish smoked sweet paprika (pimentón dulce)

½ teaspoon dried thyme

410-g/14-oz. can chickpeas, rinsed and well drained

4 handfuls of baby spinach leaves

250 g/9 oz. cherry tomatoes, halved

2 tablespoons freshly squeezed lemon juice

sea salt and freshly ground black pepper

a ridged stove-top grill pan or heavy cast iron frying pan

Serves 4

Preheat a grill pan over high heat.

Trim the crusts off the bread and discard. Brush both sides of the bread lightly with some of the oil. Add to the preheated pan and cook until golden and slightly charred on both sides. Rub the garlic cloves over the toasted bread and let cool. Tear into large chunks and set aside.

Heat the remaining oil in the pan. Add the chorizo slices and stir-fry for 2–3 minutes, until golden and aromatic. Add the onion, paprika and thyme and cook for 2–3 minutes, until softened. Transfer to a large bowl and pour in the seasoned oil from the pan. Add the toasted bread, chickpeas, spinach, tomatoes and lemon juice. Season to taste with salt and pepper and toss well to combine. Serve immediately.

Vegetarian option: Smoked tofu makes a good substitute for the chorizo here and tofu or organic vegetarian sausages also work well, if you can find a brand that you like. Simply cook separately, slice and add to the finished dish.

Mexican taco salad with pinto beans and avocado

The fresh flavours of tomato, avocado and coriander/cilantro form the basis of Mexican cuisine and are combined here in a nutritious salad with little pinto beans and crunchy taco pieces. I find canned pinto beans difficult to source so prefer to soak and cook my own, but if you'd rather use canned beans, kidney beans can be substituted. This is a rather dry salad as it keeps the taco pieces crisp but if you want a dressing, simply add a little good olive oil combined with freshly squeezed lime juice.

150 g/¾ cup dried pinto beans

2 firm, ripe avocados

3 ripe tomatoes

50 g/⅓ cup pitted black olives, sliced

1 red onion, thinly sliced

1 crisp lettuce, such as iceberg, shredded

leaves from a small bunch of fresh coriander/cilantro, roughly chopped

8 stoneground yellow corn taco shells (preferably organic)

Serves 4

Put the beans in a bowl, cover with cold water and let soak overnight.

Drain the beans and cook in a large saucepan of boiling water for 3–3½ hours, until tender, topping up the water from time to time. Drain well and transfer to a large bowl.

Preheat the oven to 180°C (350°F) Gas 4.

Cut the avocados in half and remove the pits. Use a tablespoon to scoop out the flesh in one piece and slice the flesh into wedges. Put it in the bowl with the beans.

Cut the tomatoes in half, squeeze out and discard as many seeds as possible and thinly slice the flesh. Put in the bowl with the beans and avocados. Add the olives, onion, lettuce and coriander/cilantro and gently toss to combine.

Put the taco shells on a baking sheet and cook in the preheated oven for 8–10 minutes, until crisp. When cool enough to handle, roughly break each taco shell into pieces and add to the bowl of salad. Toss to combine, being careful not to break up the taco pieces, and serve immediately.

hot smoked salmon and cannellini bean salad with gremolata

Gremolata is a zesty mixture of parsley, lemon and garlic, sometimes combined with olive oil, which is used in many classic Italian dishes. Here it is used to balance the richness of hot smoked salmon. The addition of buttery cannellini beans make this a delicious and satisfying salad.

leaves from a bunch each of fresh flat leaf parsley and fresh mint, roughly chopped

1 clove garlic, crushed

1 teaspoon finely grated lemon zest

2 tablespoons freshly squeezed lemon juice

65 ml/¼ cup extra virgin olive oil

400 g/14 oz. hot smoked salmon fillet

410-g/14 oz. can cannellini beans, drained and well rinsed

2 small red onions, thinly sliced

1 cucumber, peeled, split lengthways, deseeded and sliced into crescents

2 handfuls baby spinach leaves

sea salt and freshly ground black pepper

Serves 4

Combine the parsley, mint, garlic, lemon zest and juice and oil in a small bowl.

Roughly flake the salmon into a large bowl and add the beans, onions, cucumber and spinach leaves. Season to taste with salt and pepper and toss to combine. Serve immediately with the gremolata on the side as a spooning sauce.

Vegetarian option: Replace the salmon with 400 g/14-oz. firm tofu or tempeh (an Indonesian speciality that has a nuttier, more savoury flavour than tofu), cut into thin slivers, and add a handful of roughly chopped fresh coriander/cilantro leaves for extra flavour.

herbed aubergine, chilli and cannellini bean salad

Aubergine/eggplant acts like a sponge and soaks up other flavours. Here it is chargrilled and tossed in a delicious spicy herb dressing.

2 large aubergines/eggplants, trimmed

2 tablespoons light olive oil

410-g/14-oz. can cannellini beans, drained and well rinsed

4 handfuls of wild rocket/arugula

herb dressing:

3 tablespoons olive oil

a handful of fresh basil leaves

a handful of fresh flat leaf parsley leaves

1 tablespoon finely chopped fresh dill

1 large fresh red chilli, deseeded and finely chopped

2 garlic cloves, chopped

1 tablespoon red wine vinegar

Serves 4

To make the dressing, put the oil, basil, parsley, dill, chilli and garlic in a food processor and process until combined. Stir in the vinegar. Set aside.

Thinly slice the aubergines/eggplants lengthways. Brush a stove-top grill pan or large non-stick frying pan lightly with some of the oil and heat until hot. Cook the aubergine/eggplant slices for 2–3 minutes on each side, until golden and crisp. Put the cooked aubergine/eggplant in a bowl and while it is still warm drizzle over a few teaspoons of the dressing, tossing to coat. Continue until all the aubergine/eggplant slices and dressing have been used.

Transfer the aubergine/eggplant to a large bowl. Add the beans, rocket/arugula and remaining oil. Toss to combine and serve immediately.

Greek salad with butter beans

This is a slight twist on a classic Greek salad. Butter beans are a staple of Greek cuisine but are usually served baked in a rich tomato sauce and served as part of a meze. Their delicate flavour works well here with tangy feta and olives. Let sit at room temperature for half an hour before serving.

400 g/14 oz. cherry tomatoes, halved

50 g/½ cup kalamata olives, halved and pitted

leaves from a small bunch of fresh mint, roughly chopped

leaves from a small bunch of fresh flat leaf parsley, finely chopped

2 x 410-g/14-oz. cans butter beans, drained and well rinsed

3 tablespoons olive oil

2 red onions, thinly sliced

2 garlic cloves, finely chopped

3 tablespoons freshly squeezed lemon juice

200 g/7 oz. feta cheese, cut into cubes

sea salt and freshly ground black pepper

bread, to serve

Serves 4

Put the tomatoes, olives, mint, parsley and beans in a large bowl and toss to combine.

Put the oil in a frying pan set over medium heat. Add the onions and garlic. When they start to sizzle in the oil, remove from the heat and pour over the tomato mixture. Stir in the lemon juice and add the feta. Season to taste with salt and pepper and toss well to combine. Serve at room temperature with bread.

lentil and artichoke salad with salsa verde

I make this salsa verde often and spoon it over rare roast beef, grilled chicken, smoked salmon or grilled tuna steaks. The capers, anchovies and pickles have a long shelf life so don't be put off by the long list of ingredients. I have cheated here and used deli-bought chargrilled artichokes, but you could also use good-quality canned ones, which make this quick and simple to prepare. Try any leftovers on bruschetta that has been spread with soft goat's cheese or ricotta.

200 g/1 cup Puy lentils
400 g/14 oz. chargrilled artichokes, quartered

salsa verde:
a handful of fresh mint leaves
a handful of fresh flat leaf parsley leaves
a handful of fresh basil leaves
2 teaspoons salted capers, rinsed
2 anchovy fillets in oil (optional)
2 garlic cloves
1 pickled gherkin (about 5 cm/2 inches long)
3 tablespoons olive oil
1 tablespoon red wine vinegar
2 teaspoons Dijon mustard

Serves 4

To make the salsa verde, put all the ingredients in a food processor and process until you have a chunky green sauce. Set aside.

Cook the lentils in a large saucepan of boiling water for about 30 minutes, until tender yet still firm to the bite. Drain well and transfer to a large bowl. Add the artichokes and stir in the salsa. Serve soon after making as the salsa will quickly lose its colour.

black-eyed bean and red pepper salad with warm halloumi

I have yet to enjoy cold, uncooked halloumi cheese – it really needs to be fried until golden in olive oil before being added to salads or enjoyed as part of a meze. It turns rubbery soon after cooking so serve this salad as quickly as possible after making. If you can find bottled Spanish-style roasted peppers (pimientos) in oil, do use these in the salad as they will add extra flavour.

300 g/1½ cups dried black-eyed beans (cow peas)
3 fresh plum tomatoes (such as Roma), diced
1 red bell pepper, deseeded and diced
leaves from a bunch of fresh coriander/cilantro, chopped
65 m/¼ cup olive oil
200 g/7 oz. halloumi cheese, cut into 2.5-cm/1-inch pieces
2 tablespoons freshly squeezed lemon juice
1 tablespoon red wine vinegar
sea salt and freshly ground black pepper

Serves 4

Put the beans in a bowl, cover with cold water and let soak overnight.

Drain the beans and cook in a large saucepan of boiling water for 1–1½ hours, until tender. Drain and transfer to a large bowl. Add the tomatoes, red pepper, coriander/cilantro and half of the oil.

Heat the remaining oil in a non-stick frying pan set over high heat. Add the halloumi and cook for 3–4 minutes, turning often, until golden brown all over. Add to the bowl with the tomato mixture and stir in the lemon juice and vinegar. Season to taste and serve immediately.

quinoa tabbouleh

Quinoa (pronounced keen-wah) *has been grown for thousands of years. The ancient Peruvians called it the 'mother of all grains'. It is very high in protein and can be used like couscous, rice or as a substitute for cracked wheat or bulgur, as in this recipe.*

150 g/¾ cup quinoa
3 ripe tomatoes
1 cucumber
4 spring onions/scallions, thinly sliced
leaves from a large bunch of fresh flat leaf parsley
leaves from a small bunch of fresh mint

dressing:
85 ml/⅓ cup freshly squeezed lemon juice
1 teaspoon sea salt
65 ml/¼ cup olive oil

Serves 4

To make the dressing, combine the lemon juice and salt in a small bowl. When the salt has dissolved, whisk in the oil. Set aside.

Put the quinoa in a saucepan and add 500 ml/2 cups cold water. Set over high heat and bring to the boil. Reduce the heat to a low simmer and cook for about 5 minutes, until the grains are just cooked. Rinse under cold water and drain well. Set aside.

Cut the tomatoes in half, squeeze out as many seeds as possible and discard. Chop the flesh into small dice. Cut the cucumber in half lengthways, scoop out the seeds and cut the cucumber into small dice, about the same size as the tomatoes. Combine the quinoa, tomatoes, cucumber, spring onions/scallions, parsley, mint and dressing in a bowl and stir until well combined. Serve immediately.

quinoa, corn and tuna salad

This is a really delicious and healthy salad and one that the kids will love.

150 g/¾ cup quinoa
1 tablespoon butter
65 ml/¼ cup olive oil
2 cobs/ears of fresh (sweet)corn, husked
2 tablespoons freshly snipped chives
leaves from a small bunch of fresh flat leaf parsley, finely chopped
leaves from a small bunch of fresh coriander/cilantro, finely chopped
1 butterhead/Boston (soft) lettuce, leaves separated
390-g/15-oz. can tuna, drained
1 tablespoon white wine vinegar
sea salt and freshly ground black pepper

Serves 4

Put the quinoa in a saucepan and add 500 ml/2 cups cold water. Set over high heat and bring to the boil. Reduce the heat to a low simmer and cook for about 5 minutes, until the grains are just cooked through. Rinse under cold water and drain well.

Put the butter and 1 tablespoon of the oil in a non-stick frying pan and set over high heat. Cook the corn cobs/ears for 8–10 minutes, turning every 2 minutes until golden all over. When cool enough to handle, shuck the corn kernels from the cobs/ears and put in a large bowl. Add the quinoa, chives, parsley, coriander/cilantro and lettuce. Roughly flake the tuna and add to the salad. Gently toss to combine.

Whisk the remaining oil and vinegar together in a small bowl. Pour over the salad and toss well. Season to taste with salt and pepper and serve immediately.

Vegetarian option: Replace the tuna with crumbled feta or grated Cheddar cheese.

poached chicken and brown rice salad with ginger and lime

I am so glad that brown rice has come out of the back of the kitchen cupboard and is no longer perceived as 'hippie food'. It has a deliciously nutty and wholesome texture and combined here with Asian flavourings, such as tamari, sesame oil, lime and spicy ginger, it gets a new lease of life.

220 g/1 cup short grain brown rice

1 tablespoon sea salt

5-cm/2-inch piece of fresh ginger, peeled

2 spring onions/scallions

a small bunch of fresh coriander/cilantro

2 skinless chicken breast fillets

leaves from a small bunch of fresh mint

1 tablespoon sesame oil

65 ml/¼ cup tamari or dark soy sauce

2 tablespoons freshly squeezed lime juice

1 teaspoon sugar

lime wedges, to serve

Serves 4

Put the rice in a large saucepan with plenty of water. Set over high heat, bring to the boil then reduce the heat and cook for about 30 minutes, until tender. Rinse under cold water, drain well and put in a bowl.

Put 3 litres/quarts cold water in a saucepan and add the salt. Cut the ginger in half. Thinly slice one half and finely grate the other. Put the sliced ginger in the saucepan with the water and put the grated ginger in a bowl. Roughly chop the spring onions/scallions (green parts only) and add to the pan. Finely chop the white parts and add to the reserved grated ginger. Cut the stems off the coriander/cilantro and add to the water. Roughly chop the coriander/cilantro leaves and add these to the rice.

Bring the water to the boil then add the chicken breasts, making sure they are fully submerged. Cover the pan with a tight-fitting lid and remove from the heat. Let the chicken poach, undisturbed, for 45 minutes. Remove from the water and let cool to room temperature.

Add the mint leaves to the rice. Add the sesame oil, tamari, lime juice and sugar to the bowl with the grated ginger and spring onion/scallion whites and stir to combine.

Thinly slice the chicken and add to the rice mixture. Add the dressing, stir to combine and serve with lime wedges for squeezing.

spiced pumpkin, spelt and goat's cheese salad

Spelt is one of the most ancient cultivated wheats – rich in vitamins and minerals and in a readily digestible form, unlike ordinary wheat. Because of its high nutritional value it has recently become more a popular choice. If you can't find pumpkin, butternut squash makes a good substitute here.

50 g/⅓ cup whole spelt

400 g/14 oz. peeled and deseeded pumpkin flesh

65 ml/¼ cup olive oil

½ teaspoon sea salt

½ teaspoon Spanish smoked sweet paprika (pimentón dulce)

¼ teaspoon dried chilli/hot pepper flakes

¼ teaspoon ground allspice

50 g/⅓ cup unsalted cashew nuts

1 tablespoon white wine vinegar

100 g/4 oz. soft goat's cheese

4 handfuls of wild rocket/arugula

freshly ground black pepper

a baking sheet lined with baking paper

Serves 4

Put the spelt in a large saucepan with plenty of boiling water. Set over high heat, bring back to the boil and cook for about 30 minutes, until just tender yet still firm to the bite. Drain well and set aside.

Preheat the oven to 180°C (350°F) Gas 4.

Cut the pumpkin flesh into large bite-sized chunks and put in a bowl with half of the oil, salt, paprika, chilli/hot pepper flakes and allspice. Toss to coat the pumpkin in the spiced oil. Tumble the pumpkin onto the prepared baking sheet and pour over any spiced oil from the bowl. Cook in the preheated oven for about 20 minutes. Remove from the oven, scatter over the cashews and return to the oven for 8–10 minutes more, until the cashews are golden and the pumpkin tender. Remove from the oven and set aside.

Combine the remaining oil and vinegar in a small bowl. Put the spelt, spiced pumpkin, cashews, goat's cheese and rocket/arugula in a large bowl and gently toss to combine, being careful not to break up the cheese or pumpkin too much. Pour over the dressing and season well with black pepper. Serve immediately.

SIDES

lemon and cardamom basmati rice

The Hindi word 'basmati' literally means 'the fragrant one', and it is considered to be the prince of rice. This recipe is from Southern India and is typically colourful, light and zesty.

300 g/1½ cups basmati rice
3 cardamom pods
½ teaspoon turmeric
2 tablespoons freshly squeezed lemon juice
3 tablespoons rice bran oil
1 tablespoon black mustard seeds
6–8 curry leaves (fresh or dried)
1 tablespoon finely grated fresh ginger
1 tablespoon finely grated lemon zest
leaves from a small bunch of fresh coriander/cilantro, finely chopped
sea salt

Serves 4

Put the rice in a sieve/strainer and rinse under cold water until the water runs clear. Transfer the rice to a large saucepan, add 750 ml/3 cups cold water and set over high heat. Add the cardamom, turmeric and a pinch of salt to the pan and stir well to combine. Bring to the boil, reduce the heat to a simmer and cook for about 20 minutes, until the rice is tender. Drain well and transfer to a large bowl. Stir in the lemon juice.

Heat the oil in a small saucepan set over high heat. Add the mustard seeds and cook until they pop. Stir in the curry leaves and ginger and cook for 1 minute. Pour the oil and spices over the rice and stir well to combine. Stir in the lemon zest and coriander/cilantro just before serving.

tamari brown rice with pumpkin seeds

This is a really wholesome recipe, and a very simple one too. Tamari is used here; it is similar to dark soy sauce in flavour but made without wheat, a common ingredient in the fermentation of soy sauce. It can be used as a substitute for soy in many recipes, such as marinades, dressings and dipping sauces, and as a general condiment for many Asian-style dishes.

50 g/½ cup pumpkin seeds (pepitas)
2 tablespoons tamari or dark soy sauce
1 tablespoon sesame oil
½ teaspoon (caster) sugar
½ teaspoon sea salt
285 g/1⅓ cups long grain brown rice

Serves 4

Dry fry the pumpkin seeds in a small frying pan set over low heat, until just golden. Set aside.

Put the tamari, sesame oil, sugar and salt in a bowl. Stir until the sugar and salt have dissolved.

Fill a large saucepan with water and set over high heat. Bring to the boil and add the rice. Stir a few times, then reduce the heat to a simmer and cook for 25 minutes, until tender.

Drain well and while still warm stir in the tamari mixture until well combined. Sprinkle the toasted pumpkin seeds over the top just before serving.

Southern-style red beans and rice

This dish typifies southern American cooking, particularly that of Louisiana, and is Creole in origin. My recipe is not entirely traditional as it's a dish that can sometimes be stodgy and unappealing, so my version is lighter but still very tasty. I've used kidney beans but smaller South Louisiana red beans could be used if you can find some. This recipe would almost always include leftover pork, ham or sausage so do add if you have some to hand.

300 g/1½ cups dried kidney beans

2 onions

4 cloves

2 sprigs of fresh thyme

1 bay leaf

2 tablespoons rice bran oil

2 garlic cloves, finely chopped

300 g/1½ cups jasmine rice

700 ml/3 cups vegetable stock

a small bunch of fresh coriander/cilantro, finely chopped

sea salt and freshly ground black pepper

Serves 4

Soak the beans in cold water overnight. Drain and transfer to a large saucepan.

Peel one of the onions and push the cloves firmly into the flesh. Put the onion in the saucepan with the beans, along with the thyme sprigs and bay leaf. Set over high heat and cover with 2 litres/quarts cold water. Bring to the boil, reduce the heat to a medium simmer and cook for about 1½–2 hours, topping up with a little extra water if necessary, until the beans are tender. Drain well, discarding the onion and herbs.

Finely chop the remaining onion. Heat the oil in a large saucepan set over high heat. Add the onion and garlic and cook for 4–5 minutes, until golden. Add the rice and cook for 1 minute, until glossy and shiny. Add the stock, letting it sizzle and boil. Reduce the heat to a low simmer, cover with a tight-fitting lid and cook for 15 minutes. Fluff the rice up and stir in the beans and coriander/cilantro. Season to taste with salt and pepper. Serve whilst hot.

Moroccan-spiced brown rice with almonds and currants

Here is a deliciously different rice dish with plenty of flavour and texture thanks to the addition of sweet currants and toasted almonds. Serve as a side dish with any roasted meats, grilled chicken or fish or as part of a cold buffet.

285 g/1⅓ cups long grain brown rice

50 g/⅓ cup currants

1 cinnamon stick

65 ml/¼ cup olive oil

2 red onions, thinly sliced

1 teaspoon ground cumin

½ teaspoon sea salt

50 g/⅓ cup flaked almonds or shelled unsalted pistachios

2 tablespoons freshly squeezed lemon juice

1 large fresh red chilli, deseeded and finely chopped

Serves 4

Put the rice, currants and cinnamon stick in a large saucepan and add 750 ml/3 cups cold water. Stir to combine and set over high heat. Bring to the boil, reduce the heat to a low simmer, cover with a tight-fitting lid and cook for 45 minutes, until the rice is tender.

Fluff the rice up with a fork to separate as many grains as possible. Remove from the heat, recover with the lid and let sit for a further 5 minutes. Discard the cinnamon stick. Tip the rice into a large bowl and let cool.

Heat the oil in a frying pan set over high heat. Add the onions, cumin and salt and cook for 8–10 minutes, until the onions are crisp, golden and aromatic. Let cool, then stir into the rice.

Dry fry the almonds in a small frying pan set over low heat, until just golden. Stir into the rice mixture along with the lemon juice and chilli. Serve at room temperature or chilled, as preferred.

Tuscan beans with fresh sage

This recipe is what cooking with dried pulses is all about – the herbs infuse the water in which the beans are cooked and add plenty of flavour. Simple.

400 g/14-oz. dried cannellini
or haricot/navy beans

2 sprigs of fresh sage

1 fresh bay leaf

1 head garlic, cloves separated

65 ml/¼ cup extra virgin olive oil

leaves from a small bunch of fresh
flat leaf parsley, finely chopped

1 teaspoon sea salt

Serves 4

Soak the beans in water overnight. Drain and put in a large saucepan along with the sage, bay leaf and garlic cloves. Cover with cold water and set over high heat. Bring to the boil and cook for about 1¼ hours, until the beans are tender. Drain and discard the sage, bay leaf and garlic. Stir in the oil, parsley and salt and serve warm.

baked inside-out stuffing with wild rice, pine nuts and raisins

Wild rice is not really rice at all, but an aquatic grass that grows in marshy areas around the North American Great Lakes and was once a favourite food of the native Americans. As it's quite expensive, it's often served mixed with long grain rice, as here, to which it adds a deliciously chewy contrast in texture. I refer to this recipe as 'inside out' stuffing as although you could use it as you would a conventional stuffing mixture (in a chicken or a rolled loin of pork, for example) cooked this way it can be served as a side dish to both vegetarians and non-veggies. It makes a really great accompaniment to a Christmas roast turkey.

50 g/¼ cup wild rice

50 g/¼ cup long grain white rice

2 tablespoons butter

2 tablespoons olive oil

1 onion, finely chopped

1 carrot, grated

1 celery stick, finely chopped

2 garlic cloves, finely chopped

50 g/½ cup stale breadcrumbs

100 g/⅔ cup raisins

50 g/⅓ cup pine nuts

1 egg, beaten

150 ml/⅔ cup vegetable stock

2–3 tablespoons extra virgin olive oil

sea salt

a medium baking dish, well buttered

Serves 4

Bring a large saucepan of water to the boil. Add the wild rice and cook for 25 minutes. Add the white rice to the water and cook for a further 10–15 minutes, until both rices are tender. Drain well and transfer to a large bowl.

Preheat the oven to 180°C (350°F) Gas 4.

Heat the butter and oil in a large frying pan set over medium heat. When the butter is sizzling, add the onion, carrot, celery, garlic and a pinch of salt and cook for 8–10 minutes, until softened. Add this mixture to the rice along with the breadcrumbs, raisins, pine nuts, egg and stock and mix well to thoroughly combine.

Spoon the mixture into the prepared baking dish and gently press down to compact. Drizzle over the olive oil and cook in the preheated oven for 45 minutes, until golden on top. Serve warm as a side dish.

spicy coconut daal

This recipe is very mushy, almost soup-like, as the lentils soften and absorb the flavours of the spices. If you are lucky enough to find fresh curry leaves, buy heaps and store them in an airtight bag in the fridge.

3 tablespoons rice bran oil

2 onions

2 fresh green chillies, deseeded and chopped

¼ teaspoon ground turmeric

½ teaspoon ground cumin

225 g/1¼ cups dried split red lentils

250 ml/1 cup coconut milk

1 tomato, chopped

1 teaspoon cumin seeds

½ teaspoon black mustard seeds

6–8 curry leaves (preferably fresh but dried are fine)

Serves 4

Heat 1 tablespoon of the oil in a saucepan set over medium heat. Chop one of the onions and add to the pan with the chillies. Cook for 4–5 minutes, until softened. Stir in the turmeric and ground cumin and cook for 1 minute more, until aromatic.

Increase the heat to high. Add the lentils, coconut milk, tomato and 750 ml/3 cups water. Bring to the boil, then reduce the heat to a low simmer and cook for 25–30 minutes, stirring often, until the lentils are very soft and mushy. Reduce the heat to very low.

Heat the remaining oil in a small saucepan set over medium heat. Add the cumin and mustard seeds and cook until they start to pop. Finely chop the remaining onion and add to the pan along with the curry leaves. Cook for 2–3 minutes, until the onions are just soft. Stir this mixture into the lentils and cook for 2 minutes. Serve whilst hot.

mujaddarah

This is wonderful comfort food that is eaten all over the Middle East, especially in Syria and the Lebanon. It is basically a one-pot dish of spiced rice and lentils, though recipes vary from region to region. You can stir in some garden peas or shelled broad/fava beans for extra colour.

65 ml/¼ cup olive oil

2 onions, thinly sliced

2 teaspoons cumin seeds

240 g/1⅓ cups dried green lentils

2 bay leaves

140 g/¾ cup basmati rice

leaves from a small bunch of fresh coriander/cilantro, roughly chopped

sea salt

Serves 4

Heat the oil in a frying pan set over medium heat. Add the onions, cumin and a generous pinch of salt. Cook for 8–10 minutes, stirring often, until soft and golden. Remove from the heat.

Bring a large saucepan of water to the boil. Add the lentils and bay leaves, reduce the heat to a medium simmer and cook for 15 minutes. Add the rice, stir, and cook for about 15–20 minutes, until both the lentils and rice are tender. Drain well and transfer to a large bowl. Stir in half of the onion mixture and the coriander/cilantro.

Return the pan with the remaining onion mixture to high heat and cook until dark golden and crispy. Spoon the crispy onion mixture over the lentils and serve hot.

Puy lentils with bacon

The tiny, dark blue-green Puy lentil grows in the volcanic soil of the Auvergne region in central France. They are considered to be far superior in taste and texture to other lentil varieties and hold their bead-like shape when cooked. They are perfect for this simple dish, where you want to retain a nutty bite and not cook the lentils down to a soft purée, as you would for Indian daals.

300 g/1½ cups Puy lentils
65 ml/¼ cup olive oil
100 g/3 slices streaky bacon, diced
1 onion, finely chopped
2 garlic cloves, crushed
2 tablespoons red wine vinegar
1 tablespoon freshly squeezed lemon juice
a handful of fresh flat leaf parsley leaves, roughly chopped
2 tablespoons finely chopped fresh mint leaves
a small bunch of chives, snipped
sea salt and freshly ground black pepper

Serves 4

Put the lentils in a saucepan with 1 litre/4 cups cold water and set over high heat. Bring to the boil, then reduce the heat to a low simmer. Cook for about 25 minutes, until tender yet still firm to the bite. Drain well.

Heat the oil in a large frying pan set over medium heat. Add the bacon and cook for about 5 minutes, until golden and crisp. Add the onion and cook for 2–3 minutes, until softened. Stir in the garlic and cook for 1 minute more. Add the cooked lentils, vinegar, lemon juice, parsley, mint and chives and mix well to combine. Season to taste with salt and pepper and serve warm rather than piping hot.

Iranian rice

This is a simple and novel way of cooking rice. If you have ever cooked potato rösti, this will be dead easy. Pre-cooked rice is cooked in a frying pan with butter, forming a large disc shape and frying the rice on the bottom side to a crisp golden brown. Tipped out onto a large plate, it makes for easy serving. Serve with stews, curries and casseroles.

450 g/2¼ cups white long grain rice
125 g/1 stick unsalted butter, melted

Serves 4–6

Put the rice in a sieve/strainer and rinse under cold water until the water runs clear. Drain well.

Bring a large saucepan of water to the boil. Add the rice and cook for 10 minutes, until the rice is firm to the bite. Drain well and let cool.

Put half of the butter in a large, non-stick frying pan and set over high heat. Swirl the pan around to coat it in the melting butter. When the butter is sizzling, add the rice and gently press the rice into the pan using the back of a large metal spoon or a potato masher.

Using the handle of a wooden spoon, make 8–10 small holes or divets in the rice. Melt the remaining butter and pour it into the holes, then pour 65 ml/¼ cup water over the rice. Reduce the heat to low, cover the frying pan with a tight-fitting lid or with foil and cook for 20–25 minutes. Let the rice cool in the pan for 10 minutes. Shake the pan a couple of times to help remove any stuck on bits.

Take a plate slightly larger than the frying pan and sit it on top. Carefully tip the frying pan upside-down onto the plate, inverting the rice so that the golden cooked grains are now on top. Serve in slices with curries, casseroles and stews.

Vietnamese 'red' rice

In my hometown of Sydney, Vietnamese restaurants flourish and are well on their way to overtaking Thai as the most popular style of Asian cuisine. You will not see this in all Vietnamese restaurants but whenever I do, I order it. It's a little like a Chinese-style fried rice, but not as substantial; I could eat that as a meal in its own right! The Vietnamese would serve this with a wonderful crispy-skinned chicken. This has inspired me to have this tomato rice as a side to a Sunday roast chicken along with an Asian-style coleslaw.

265 g/1⅓ cups white long grain rice
670 ml/2¾ cups vegetable stock
3 tablespoons sunflower oil
3 garlic cloves, crushed
2 tablespoons tomato purée/paste
2 tablespoons butter
1 tablespoon light soy sauce

Serves 4

Put the rice in a sieve/strainer and rinse under cold water until the water runs clear. Drain well.

Put the stock and the rice in a large saucepan and bring to the boil. As soon as the stock boils, cover with a tight-fitting lid and reduce the heat to low. Simmer for 10 minutes.

Spread the rice out on a large baking sheet and refrigerate for 6 hours, or overnight, turning the rice several times so it dries out. Remove the rice from the refrigerator 30 minutes before cooking.

Heat a wok or large non-stick frying pan over high heat. Add the oil, swirling the pan around to coat the base and sides in oil. Add the garlic and cook for a few seconds without burning, just to flavour the oil. Add the rice and stir fry for 2–3 minutes, using a large spoon to break up any large clumps of rice, separating as many grains as possible.

Stir in the tomato purée/paste until it is evenly distributed throughout the rice, turning it red.

Stir in the butter and soy sauce and serve hot.

buttered buckwheat with sweetcorn

Nutty, earthy buckwheat (kasha) is a staple food in Eastern Europe, as well as in Russia, where the grain is milled into a speckled grey flour and used to make mini pancakes (blinis). Unusually, buckwheat is a complete protein, containing all eight amino acids.

2 tablespoons butter
1 tablespoon sunflower oil
2 cobs/ears of fresh (sweet)corn, shucked
150 g/1 cup buckwheat/kasha
(roasted buckwheat groats)
1 egg, beaten
500 ml/2 cups vegetable stock
a handful of fresh flat leaf parsley leaves, chopped
a handful of fresh basil leaves, chopped
1 tablespoon finely chopped fresh dill
1 tablespoon finely snipped chives
sea salt and freshly ground black pepper

Serves 4

Heat the butter and oil in a frying pan set over medium heat. When the butter is sizzling, add the (sweet)corn kernels and a pinch of salt to the pan and cook for 2–3 minutes, until the (sweet)corn is shiny and glossy. Set aside.

Put the buckwheat in a bowl and stir in the beaten egg so that the grains are well coated. Tip the buckwheat mixture into a non-stick frying pan and set over high heat. Cook for 2–3 minutes, stirring constantly, until the buckwheat looks dry. Add the stock and quickly stir to combine. Reduce the heat to medium/low and cook for 10 minutes, until the stock is absorbed and the buckwheat is tender. Remove from the heat. Add the (sweet)corn mixture and herbs and season to taste with salt and pepper. Mix well to combine and serve hot.

spiced buttered couscous

Couscous is made by steaming and drying cracked durum wheat. It is the national dish in Morocco where the traditional way to cook it is to set the grains over a stew and steam it, which requires considerable time and preparation. Luckily for us, pre-cooked couscous is widely available and could not be easier to prepare. Here, this simple accompaniment is taken to another level with the addition of warming spices.

½ teaspoon ground cumin
½ teaspoon sweet paprika
¼ teaspoon ground ginger
¼ teaspoon chilli powder
225 g/1½ cups couscous
2 tablespoons butter, cut into cubes

Serves 4

Combine the cumin, paprika, ginger and chilli powder in a small frying pan and set over medium heat. Shake the pan until the spices are aromatic and starting to smoke, but not burning. Remove from the heat and set aside.

Put the couscous in a heatproof bowl. Add the toasted spices and scatter the cubed butter over the top. Pour in 375 ml/1½ cups hot water, quickly stirring a couple of times, then cover the bowl tightly with clingfilm/plastic wrap. Let sit for 10 minutes. Use a fork to fluff up the grains, then cover and lit sit for 5 minutes more.

Finally, tip the couscous into a larger bowl and fluff up the grains with your fingertips, separating as many grains as possible for a light-as-air result. Serve warm as an accompaniment.

MAIN DISHES

slow-cooked pork belly with soya beans and miso

In China, soya beans are known as the 'meat of the earth' because of their high nutritional value. They are, however, quite bland and need plenty of robust ingredients with distinctive flavours cooking alongside them. The Asian flavours I've used here do the job nicely.

100 g/⅔ cup dried soya beans

1 kg/2¼ lbs. pork belly, in 1 piece

125 ml/½ cup sake (Japanese rice wine)

1 tablespoon peanut oil

2 teaspoons sesame oil

3 garlic cloves, roughly chopped

4 spring onions/scallions, white parts only, chopped

5 thin slices fresh ginger

250 ml/1 cup chicken or vegetable stock

2 tablespoons light soy sauce

2 tablespoons white miso/shinshu (soya bean paste)

1 teaspoon sugar

½ teaspoon sea salt

a large, flameproof casserole

Serves 4

Soak the soya beans in 750 ml/3 cups cold water for at least 10 hours or overnight. Drain well and transfer to a large saucepan.

Add plenty of boiling water and set the pan over medium heat. Cook for 45–50 minutes, until the beans are tender. Drain and set aside.

Cut the pork belly into 8 pieces. Put the pieces in a dish and pour over the sake. Cover with clingfilm/plastic wrap and set aside for 1 hour, turning often. Remove the pork from the sake, reserving the sake.

Put the peanut oil in a flameproof casserole and set over high heat. Cook the pork in batches (so as not to overcrowd the pan), for 4–5 minutes, turning often until golden all over. Put the browned pork in a bowl and set aside.

Preheat the oven to 160°C (325°F) Gas 3.

Add the sesame oil to the casserole. Add the garlic, spring onions/scallions and ginger and stir-fry for 1–2 minutes, until aromatic and softened. Add the reserved sake, letting it boil, and cook until the liquid has reduced by half, stirring to remove any stuck-on bits of pork from the bottom of the casserole. Add the stock, soy sauce, miso/shinshu, sugar and salt and return the pork to the pan, stirring until the miso/shinshu dissolves. Bring to the boil, cover with a tight-fitting lid, transfer to the preheated oven and cook for 2 hours, turning the pork after 1 hour. Stir in the soya beans, cover and cook for 30 minutes more. Serve hot.

bean and pork ragù with tagliatelle

Broad/fava beans have an almost meaty flavour and texture and I guess this is why they have played such an important role in the diet of people in cultures where meat was beyond the means of most people. They often form the basis of rustic country dishes, such as this Italian-influenced recipe.

50 g/3 tablespoons butter

1 white onion, chopped

2 garlic cloves, finely chopped

1 carrot, finely chopped

1 celery stick, finely chopped

100 g/4 oz. pancetta, finely chopped

400 g/14 oz. boneless pork shoulder, diced

2 teaspoons finely chopped fresh oregano leaves

a pinch of freshly ground nutmeg

125 ml/½ cup white wine

250 ml/1 cup beef stock

400-g/14-oz. can chopped tomatoes

410-g/14-oz. can brown broad/fava beans, well drained and rinsed

400 g/14 oz. dried egg tagliatelle

sea salt and freshly ground black pepper

freshly grated Parmesan cheese, to serve

a flameproof casserole

Serves 4

Melt the butter in a heavy-based casserole set over high heat. Add the onion, garlic, carrot, celery and pancetta and cook for 8–10 minutes, stirring, until the vegetables have softened.

Add the diced pork, oregano and nutmeg and stir-fry for 5 minutes, until the pork is lightly browned all over.

Add the wine and let it sizzle for 2 minutes, until it is almost absorbed. Add the stock, tomatoes and 125 ml/½ cup cold water and bring to the boil. Reduce the heat to a low simmer, partially cover and cook for 1½ hours, until the pork is very tender.

Stir in the beans. Using a potato masher, mash the ingredients in the pan, so the pork breaks up and some of the beans are smashed. Season to taste with salt and pepper and cook over low heat while you cook the pasta.

Cook the tagliatelle according to the packet instructions and drain well. Tip the pasta into the ragù and toss well to combine. Serve immediately with grated Parmesan for sprinkling.

Vegetarian option: Omit the pancetta and pork shoulder and adjust the cooking time accordingly. Keep the quantity of broad/fava beans the same and add a bay leaf and a sprig of fresh thyme for extra flavour. Use vegetable stock in place of the beef stock.

pork sausage, fennel and bean stew

My local butcher supplies pork sausages flavoured with fennel seeds. This is a very Sicilian idea and they are so good! Other gourmet flavoured sausages, such as lamb and rosemary, would be tasty in this recipe too. Haricot/navy beans are small, white oval beans that become very tender when cooked, but cannellini beans would work just as well if that's what you have to hand. This is delicious served with soft polenta, mashed potatoes or crusty bread – basically something to mop up the delicious sauce.

2 tablespoons olive oil

12 small pork sausages

1 white onion, chopped

1 fennel bulb, chopped

2 garlic cloves, chopped

½ teaspoon fennel seeds

410-g/14-oz. can haricot/navy beans, well drained and rinsed

400-g/14-oz. can chopped tomatoes

2 teaspoons brown sugar

sea salt and freshly ground black pepper

soft polenta or mashed potatoes, to serve

Serves 4

Heat the oil in a large, heavy-based frying pan set over medium heat. Add half of the sausages to the pan and cook for 4–5 minutes, turning often, until well browned all over. Remove from the pan and repeat with the remaining sausages, removing them from the pan once browned.

Add the onion, fennel, garlic and fennel seeds to the pan and stir-fry for 5 minutes, until the fennel is softened and golden.

Add the beans, tomatoes and sugar to the pan and stir to combine. Return the sausages to the pan and bring to the boil. Reduce the heat to a low simmer and cook for 10–15 minutes. Season to taste with salt and pepper and serve with the side dish of your choice.

Vegetarian option: Try using herbed vegetarian sausages and cook exactly as you would the pork ones. I would also be tempted to add a bit of spicy heat, such as a good sprinkling of dried chilli/hot pepper flakes or a finely chopped fresh red chilli with the onions.

smoky bean and lamb casserole

Haricot/navy beans feature in many casseroles from Spain, Portugal and South America and are the beans most commonly used to make canned baked beans. The beans cook and soften in the pot in this recipe and are infused with the herbs and seasonings with delicious results. The addition of plenty of Spanish smoked sweet paprika (pimentón dulce) is what gives this dish its tantalizingly smoky flavour as well as a deep red sauce.

2 tablespoons olive oil

500 g/1 lb. lamb shoulder meat, cut into large chunks (about 4–5 cm/1½–2 inches square)

2 tablespoons butter

2 white onions, finely chopped

3 garlic cloves, roughly chopped

1 bay leaf

1 tablespoon fresh thyme leaves

1 tablespoon Spanish smoked paprika (pimentón dulce)

200 g/1 cup dried haricot/navy beans

2 x 400-g/14-oz. cans chopped tomatoes

2 tablespoons tomato purée/paste

leaves from a small bunch of fresh flat leaf parsley, roughly chopped

sea salt and freshly ground black pepper

lemon wedges, to serve

a large flameproof casserole

Serves 4

Heat the oil in a large, flameproof casserole set over high heat. Add the lamb chunks and cook for about 5 minutes, turning often, so the pieces are evenly browned all over. Remove from the pan and pour off all but about 1 tablespoon of the oil.

Add the butter to the casserole. When the butter is sizzling, add the onions, garlic, bay leaf and thyme leaves and stir-fry for 2–3 minutes, until the onion has softened and the herbs are aromatic.

Stir in the paprika and cook for 1 minute. Stir in the beans, tomatoes and tomato purée/paste. Return the lamb to the casserole and bring to the boil.

Reduce the heat to low, cover, and cook at a low simmer for 2 hours, stirring occasionally, until the lamb and beans are very tender. Season to taste with salt and pepper and stir in the parsley. Serve with lemon wedges for squeezing.

Vegetarian option: Turn this into a bean casserole by omitting the lamb and adding a 400-g/14-oz. can of drained chickpeas or brown lentils. Reduce the cooking time to 1 hour.

slow-cooked lamb shanks with lentils

This recipe is simply a few of my favourite ingredients thrown together in a pot and the alchemy of cooking does its magic. Make this once and you may be hooked. For a lighter dish, try chicken instead of lamb; choose some lovely Maryland cuts (thigh and drumstick), pan-sear until the skin is golden, then proceed with the recipe from there. Serve this with plenty of mashed potatoes and green beans.

100 g/½ cup dried green lentils

100 g/4 oz. pancetta or streaky bacon/ country ham, chopped

2 garlic cloves, chopped

400-g/14-oz. can chopped tomatoes

500 ml/2 cups chicken stock

250 ml/1 cup red wine

4 trimmed lamb shanks

a handful of fresh flat leaf parsley leaves, roughly chopped

sea salt and freshly ground black pepper

a large casserole or other lidded baking dish

Serves 4

Preheat the oven to 160°C (325°F) Gas 3.

Put the lentils, pancetta, garlic, tomatoes, stock and wine in a large casserole and season well with salt and pepper. Stir well to combine. Add the lamb shanks and cover with a tight-fitting lid.

Cook in the preheated oven for 1½ hours. Remove the casserole from the oven and turn the lamb shanks over. Re-cover, return to the oven and cook for 1 hour more, until the lamb is very tender. Stir in the parsley. Serve one shank per person with a generous portion of the lentils.

Hungarian goulash with beans

While there are many variations of this classic Hungarian dish there is one ingredient that defines goulash: paprika. This recipe not only has plenty of paprika, but the novel addition of broad/fava beans. Their earthy texture goes hand in hand with the warming spices and makes a very tasty dish. Serve with plain boiled rice.

4 tablespoons light olive oil

100 g/4 oz. pancetta, finely diced

2 white onions, finely chopped

2 garlic cloves, finely chopped

1 red bell pepper, deseeded and finely diced

2 carrots, finely diced

500 g/1 lb. stewing beef, diced

2 tablespoons sweet paprika (preferably Hungarian)

¼ teaspoon caraway seeds

1 tablespoon tomato purée/paste

1 litre/4 cups chicken or vegetable stock

400-g/14-oz. can broad/fava beans, drained and well rinsed

a handful of fresh flat leaf parsley leaves, roughly chopped

sea salt and freshly ground black pepper

boiled rice, to serve

a large, flameproof casserole

Serves 4

Heat 1 tablespoon of the oil in a large, flameproof casserole set over high heat. Add the pancetta and cook for 5 minutes, stirring often, until golden. Remove the pancetta from the pan and set aside.

Reduce the heat to medium. Add 1 tablespoon of the oil to the casserole, then add the onions and garlic. Cook for 5 minutes, until softened. Add the red pepper and carrots and cook for 8–10 minutes, until all the vegetables are softened and golden. Remove from the casserole.

Increase the heat to high. Add 1 further tablespoon oil to the casserole. Add half of the beef and cook for 4–5 minutes, stirring frequently, until well browned. Remove from the casserole. Add the remaining oil and beef to the casserole and repeat.

Add the paprika and caraway seeds to the casserole and stir-fry for 1 minute, until aromatic. Add the tomato purée/paste and stock and stir. Return all the ingredients to the casserole and bring to the boil. Reduce the heat to a low simmer and cook for 1½ hours, until the beef is very tender. Season to taste with salt and pepper. Stir in the beans and parsley and cook for 10 minutes to warm the beans through. Serve with plain boiled rice.

Vegetarian option: Omit the pancetta and beef and double the quantity of broad/fava beans. Cook the vegetables and make the sauce with the spices, tomato purée/paste and vegetable stock as above, but reduce the simmering time to 20 minutes. Add the canned beans and parsley and heat before serving.

'real' chili con carne

Chili con carne can be whipped up in no time using minced beef but the result is nothing like this. Chuck or stewing steak is a cut I use often as it cooks down to a beautiful tenderness (a texture nothing like minced beef) and absorbs flavourings well. Robust kidney or pinto beans are used in Mexican dishes as white beans, so popular in Italian and French cuisine, would be overwhelmed by all these heady spices.

2 tablespoons olive oil

1 red onion, chopped

2 garlic cloves, roughly chopped

1 teaspoon chilli powder

1 teaspoon ground cumin

½ teaspoon ground cinnamon

2 teaspoons dried oregano

500 g/1 lb. stewing beef (chuck steak), cut into 3–4 cm/1½ inch pieces

250 ml/1 cup beer

2 tablespoons smoked chipotle chilli paste/ chipotles in adobo

400-g/14-oz. can kidney or pinto beans, drained and well rinsed

boiled rice, to serve

Serves 4

Heat the oil in a heavy-based frying pan set over medium heat. Add the onion and garlic and cook for 4–5 minutes, until golden. Add the chilli powder, cumin, cinnamon and oregano and cook for 1 minute, until aromatic. Add the beef and stir-fry for 5 minutes until the beef is browned.

Add the beer, 250 ml/1 cup cold water, chipotle paste and beans. Bring to the boil, then reduce the heat to a low simmer. Cook for 1½ hours, stirring occasionally, until the beef is very tender and the sauce has thickened. Serve with plain boiled rice.

smoky baked beans

I make these delicious beans in my café where I spoon some of the mixture into individual ovenproof dishes, crack an egg in the centre and bake in a hot oven until the egg is just set – the perfect brunch dish. Date molasses are a Lebanese speciality, available from gourmet suppliers and worth seeking out for this dish alone.

1 smoked ham hock

1 onion, finely chopped

65 ml/¼ cup date molasses plus 1 tablespoon, or the same quantity of dark treacle

1 tablespoon English mustard powder

2 teaspoons cider vinegar

400 g/2 cups dried haricot/navy beans

½ teaspoon sea salt

sea salt and freshly ground black pepper

a large casserole

Serves 4

Preheat the oven to 150°C (300°F) Gas 2.

Put the ham hock, onion, 65 ml/¼ cup molasses, mustard powder, vinegar, dried beans and salt in a large casserole. Add 2 litres/quarts cold water, stir to combine and cover with a tight-fitting lid.

Cook in the preheated oven for 4 hours, stirring after 2 hours. Remove the lid and cook for another 1½–2 hours until the meat is falling off the bone and the beans are dark and tender. Remove the bone, shred any meat that remains on it into the beans and discard. Stir through the remaining 1 tablespoon of molasses and season to taste with salt and pepper.

Serve at room temperature as a side dish or as a meal on its own, with plenty of bread to soak up the sauce.

white fish, soya bean and baby carrot hot pot

If you happen to live in a city which has a Chinatown or even an Asian speciality food shop, do look out for Chinese earthenware pots (sand pots). They are an inexpensive item and make for addictive culinary experimentation! Made from clay and glazed inside, they can be used on both hob and in the oven, just like a conventional casserole, and are perfect for recipes such as this one.

800 g/1¾ lb. skinless white fish fillet, cut into bite-sized pieces

60 g/½ cup plain/all-purpose flour

2 tablespoons vegetable oil

2 teaspoons sesame oil

4 garlic cloves, roughly chopped

2 spring onions/scallions, white and green parts, thinly sliced on the angle

1 tablespoon grated fresh ginger

8 baby carrots or 1 large carrot, cut into bite-sized pieces

500 ml/2 cups fish or vegetable stock

1 tablespoon Thai fish sauce

400-g/14-oz. can soya beans, rinsed and drained

leaves from a small bunch of fresh coriander/cilantro, chopped

a large flameproof casserole

Serves 4

Put the fish pieces in a sieve/strainer with the flour. Toss to coat the fish in the flour and set aside.

Heat both the oils in a large, flameproof casserole set over high heat. Add the fish pieces in batches, cooking for just 1 minute on each side, until golden. Transfer the fish to a plate as you go.

Add the garlic, spring onion/scallion whites and ginger to the casserole and stir-fry for 2 minutes, scraping the base to remove any stuck-on bits. Add the carrots, stock, fish sauce and soya beans. Increase the heat and bring to the boil. Cook for 10 minutes, until the liquid has slightly reduced.

Add the fish pieces and gently stir. Reduce the heat to a low simmer and cook for 5 minutes, until the fish is opaque and cooked through.

Stir in half of the coriander/cilantro and scatter the remaining coriander/cilantro and spring onion/scallion greens over the top. Serve immediately.

Vegetarian option: Replace the fish with about 200 g/7 oz. peeled, deseeded and chopped butternut squash and 200 g/ 1 cup sliced fresh mushrooms, shiitake if available. Increase the cooking time by 5–10 minutes and cook until the squash is just tender. Use vegetable stock and omit the fish sauce.

chickpea and fresh spinach curry

I am a fan of good quality curry pastes but still feel the need to add my own individual, fresh touch when cooking with them. I usually cook off some onion, garlic and ginger and may add fresh or dried curry leaves and a couple of large red or green chillies, split lengthways. Chickpeas are popular in India and work brilliantly here in this spicy curry.

1 white onion, roughly chopped

2 garlic cloves, sliced

1 teaspoon chopped fresh ginger

1 tablespoon light olive oil

2 tablespoons mild curry paste

400-g/14-oz. can chopped tomatoes

400-g/14-oz. can chickpeas, well drained and rinsed

500 g/1 lb. fresh spinach, stalks removed and leaves chopped

a handful of fresh coriander/cilantro leaves, chopped

naan or roti bread, to serve

Serves 4

Put the onion, garlic and ginger in a food processor and process until finely chopped. Heat the oil in a frying pan set over high heat. Add the onion mixture and cook for 4–5 minutes, stirring often, until golden. Add the curry paste and stir-fry for just 2 minutes, until aromatic.

Stir in the tomatoes, 250 ml/1 cup cold water and the chickpeas. Bring to the boil, then reduce the heat to a medium simmer and cook, uncovered, for 10 minutes. Stir in the spinach and cook just until it is wilted.

Stir in the coriander/cilantro and serve with the Indian bread of your choice.

prawn and yellow split pea curry

In the recipe on the previous page I cheat a little and use a ready-made curry paste, but a basic curry is easy to make from a few storecupboard spices and a handful of fresh seasonings. The split peas used here cook down to a mushy consistency, thickening the sauce nicely.

1 large onion, roughly chopped

3 garlic cloves, chopped

5-cm/2-inch piece of fresh ginger, peeled and chopped

2 large fresh red chillies, deseeded and chopped

1 tablespoon vegetable oil

500 g/1 lb. raw king prawns/jumbo shrimp, peeled and deveined

6–8 curry leaves (dried or fresh)

½ teaspoon ground cumin

½ teaspoon turmeric

4 ripe tomatoes, roughly chopped

55 g/¼ cup dried yellow split peas

leaves from a small bunch of fresh coriander/cilantro, roughly chopped

sea salt and freshly ground black pepper

cooked basmati rice, to serve

Serves 4

Put the onion, garlic, ginger and chillies in a food processor and process to a paste.

Heat the oil in a large frying pan set over high heat. Add the prawns/shrimp and cook for just 2 minutes on each side, until pink. Remove from the pan and set aside.

Add the onion mixture to the pan and stir-fry for 5 minutes, until starting to turn golden. Add the curry leaves and cook for 1 minute. Stir in the cumin and turmeric and cook for 1 minute more, until aromatic.

Add the tomatoes, 125 ml/½ cup cold water and the split peas. Let the mixture sizzle and boil for 1 minute, then reduce the heat to a low simmer. Cook for 25–30 minutes, until the split peas are just tender and the mixture has thickened. Return the cooked prawns/shrimp to the pan and add the coriander/cilantro. Cook for 2 minutes, until the prawns/shrimp are heated through. Season well with salt and pepper and serve with basmati rice.

Vegetarian option: Dice about 400 g/14 oz. paneer (Indian cheese) and fry in a non-stick frying pan set over medium heat. Substitute for the prawns/shrimp, following the recipe as above.

mung bean and vegetable curry

Mung beans are pretty olive-coloured beans native to India and one of the most popular beans for sprouting. Once split and hulled they are yellow, have a slightly sweet flavour and become butter-soft with cooking. They are traditionally used in the Indian curry moong dhal, *which is flavoured with ground coriander, cumin, turmeric and hot cayenne pepper. I've added carrots to my recipe but you could add chopped pumpkin or butternut squash, baby new potatoes or cubes of pan-fried aubergine/eggplant.*

225 g/1 cup dried split mung beans

2 tablespoons vegetable oil

1 onion, finely chopped

2 teaspoons finely grated
fresh ginger

2 garlic cloves, finely chopped

2 fresh green chillies, deseeded
and finely chopped

8 curry leaves (dried or fresh)

¼ teaspoon ground turmeric

1 teaspoon ground cumin

2 carrots, sliced

400-g/14-oz. can chopped tomatoes

2 handfuls fresh spinach leaves,
stalks removed and leaves chopped

leaves from a small bunch of fresh
coriander/cilantro, roughly chopped

sea salt and freshly ground
black pepper

naan or roti bread, to serve

Serves 4

Put the mung beans in a large saucepan and add 1 litre/ 4 cups water. Bring to the boil, reduce the heat to a low simmer and cook for 20 minutes. Drain well and set aside.

Heat the oil in a heavy-based saucepan set over high heat. Add the onion, ginger, garlic, chillies and curry leaves. Cook for 2–3 minutes, stirring often, until the mixture is aromatic. Stir in the turmeric and cumin and cook for 1 minute more.

Add the carrot, tomatoes, mung beans and 125 ml/½ cup water and bring to the boil. Reduce the heat to a medium simmer and cook for 15 minutes, until the carrots are tender and the mung beans are soft and breaking up. Stir in the spinach and coriander/cilantro and cook for a couple of minutes, until the spinach has wilted. Season to taste with salt and pepper and serve with the Indian bread of your choice .

barley risotto with mushrooms and goat's cheese

Barley makes for an interesting substitute for rice in a risotto. It has a nutty and sweet flavour which works well here with both the mushrooms and the red wine and is offset by the creamy tang of goat's cheese.

20 g/1 oz. dried porcini mushrooms

1 litre/4 cups vegetable stock

65 ml/¼ cup red wine

50 g/3 tablespoons butter

1 tablespoon olive oil

1 leek, trimmed and thinly sliced

2 garlic cloves, chopped

330 g/1⅔ cups pearl barley

400 g/14 oz. fresh brown mushrooms, sliced

50 g/2 oz. soft goat's cheese

a small handful of fresh flat leaf parsley leaves, finely chopped

sea salt and freshly ground black pepper

Serves 4

Put the dried mushrooms in a heatproof bowl and cover with 125 ml/½ cup boiling water. Let soak for 20 minutes. Drain the mushrooms and reserve the soaking liquid. Roughly chop the mushrooms and set aside.

Combine the stock, red wine and reserved mushroom soaking liquid in a saucepan set over low heat.

Heat half of the butter and the oil in a heavy-based saucepan set over medium heat. Add the leek and garlic and cook for about 4–5 minutes, until the leek has softened. Stir in the barley and cook for 1 minute, until shiny and glossy.

Stir in both the fresh and dried mushrooms and cook for 2–3 minutes, until the mushrooms have wilted.

Add about 125 ml/½ cup of the hot stock mixture to the barley and stir constantly, until almost all the liquid has been absorbed. (This will take a little longer than cooking with risotto rice.) Continue adding the liquid a little at a time and stirring for about 45 minutes, until all the liquid has been added and the barley is tender.

Stir in the goat's cheese and remaining butter, until the cheese has melted. Season to taste with salt and pepper and sprinkle over the parsley. Serve immediately.

simple tomato and basil risotto

It's hard to beat a simple risotto made with fresh seasonal ingredients. Here summer-ripe tomatoes and sweet, liquoricy basil are stirred into buttery semi-cooked rice; the rice should be a little softened around the edges but still firm to the bite.

3 fresh plum tomatoes
1 litre/4 cups vegetable stock
65 ml/¼ cup dry vermouth
2 tablespoons butter
2 tablespoons olive oil
2 garlic cloves, chopped
1 large trimmed leek, sliced
325 g/1½ cups Arborio rice
a large handful of fresh basil leaves, roughly torn
50 g/½ cup finely grated Parmesan cheese
extra virgin olive oil, to drizzle

Serves 4

Cut the tomatoes in half and squeeze out and discard as many seeds as possible. Finely dice the flesh and set aside.

Put the stock and vermouth in a medium saucepan set over low heat. Put half of the butter and the oil in a heavy-based saucepan and set over medium heat. Add the garlic and leek and cook for 4–5 minutes, until softened. Add the rice and cook for 1 minute, until shiny and glossy.

Add about 65 ml/¼ cup of the hot stock mixture to the rice and stir constantly, until almost all of the liquid has been absorbed. Add another 65 ml/¼ cup to the pan, stirring until almost all the liquid has been absorbed. Continue adding the stock mixture a little at a time and stirring, until all the stock has been used and the rice is just tender.

Stir in the tomatoes, basil, Parmesan and remaining butter until well combined. Drizzle with olive oil and serve immediately.

Chinese Hainan chicken rice

This is actually a rather old-fashioned way to cook chicken. During the Australian summers of my childhood, a big pot of poached chicken on the hob was a familiar sight. It would be shredded and used in salads and sandwiches or stirred through soups. But we never had chicken poached with these wonderful Asian flavourings, all now readily available.

1.6 kg/3½ lb. chicken

a bunch of spring onions/scallions

8 garlic cloves, lightly smashed

10-cm/4-inch piece of fresh ginger, peeled and thinly sliced

40 g/3 tablespoons sea salt

265 g/1⅓ cups jasmine rice

a small bunch of fresh coriander/cilantro

ground white pepper

sliced tomato and cucumber, to serve

ginger sauce:

65 ml/¼ cup light soy sauce

½ teaspoon sugar

8 spring onions/scallions, thinly sliced on the angle

5-cm/2-inch piece of fresh ginger, peeled and finely grated

1 teaspoon sesame oil

2 tablespoons peanut oil

Serves 4

To make the ginger sauce, put the soy sauce, sugar, spring onions/scallions and ginger in a small heatproof bowl and stir to combine. Combine the sesame and peanut oils in a small saucepan set over high heat. When the oil is smoking hot, pour it over the spring onion/scallion mixture, stir and set aside.

Trim any excess fat from around the cavity of the chicken. Wash and pat dry.

Put 4 litres/quarts cold water in a large saucepan. Add the spring onions/scallions, garlic, ginger and salt and bring to the boil. Reduce the heat to a medium simmer and cook for 30 minutes. Reduce the heat to low and put the chicken in the water, breast-side down, making sure it is fully submerged. Let cook for 15 minutes, then cover with a tight-fitting lid and remove the pan from the heat. Leave to poach for 3 hours. Use tongs to carefully remove the chicken from the pan without tearing the skin. Transfer to a large bowl, cover and reserve the stock.

Put the rice in a sieve/strainer and rinse under cold water until the water runs clear. Combine the rice and 670 ml/2¾ cups of the reserved stock in a saucepan set over high heat and bring to the boil. When the stock boils, cover with a tight-fitting lid, reduce the heat to low and cook for 10 minutes.

Cut the chicken into 12 pieces. For each serving, put 3 pieces of chicken on a serving plate with the rice on the side. Arrange the tomato and cucumber slices on the plate. Sprinkle over the coriander/cilantro and pepper and serve with the ginger sauce in a small bowl on the side.

combination fried rice

I prefer to eat Chinese stir-fries with plain steamed or boiled rice and save this tasty rice dish for special occasions, as it really is a meal on its own. I have kept the ingredients list fairly basic – most of us will have some rice in the kitchen cupboard, so feel free to use whatever you have. You could substitute the bacon for ham and if you happen to live near an Asian speciality food shop, you could add some thinly sliced Chinese sausage or barbecue pork.

80 ml/⅓ cup peanut oil

4 eggs, beaten

16 raw king prawns/jumbo shrimp, peeled and deveined

2 garlic cloves, finely chopped

1 tablespoon grated fresh ginger

1 white onion, thinly sliced

2 rashers back bacon, chopped

100 g/1 cup fresh beansprouts

1 teaspoon white sugar

750 g/6 cups cooked white or brown long grain rice

4 shallots, thinly sliced

1 tablespoon oyster sauce

1–2 tablespoons light soy sauce

½ teaspoon sesame oil

¼ teaspoon ground white pepper

Serves 4

Heat half of the oil in a wok or very large non-stick frying pan set over high heat, carefully swirling the wok around to coat the sides in the oil. When smoking hot, add the beaten eggs. Let the eggs sizzle in the oil. When puffed around the edges, use a large wooden spoon to slowly stir the eggs until they are just set. Tip the eggs onto a chopping board. Let cool and roughly chop.

Add the remaining oil to the wok and heat. When smoking hot add the prawns/shrimp and stir-fry for 2–3 minutes, until pink. Remove from the wok, leaving the oil in the wok to reheat.

Add the garlic, ginger, onion and bacon to the wok and stir-fry for 2–3 minutes, until the onion is golden and the bacon starting to crisp. Add the beansprouts and sugar and stir-fry for just a few seconds to combine and until the beansprouts have wilted.

Add the rice, shallots, oyster sauce, soy sauce, sesame oil and pepper to the wok and stir-fry for 2–3 minutes, until well combined and the rice has heated through. Add the eggs and prawns/shrimp to the wok, stir well to combine and serve immediately.

SWEET
THINGS
& BAKING

Anzac cookies

In Australia and New Zealand these are known as Anzac biscuits and are a popular home-baked treat. I've used unprocessed whole oats here, as they have the nutritious bran and germ remaining intact. Baking them for a little less time will result in a chewy texture and cooking them for a little longer will result in a crisp cookie.

90 g/¾ cup unsweetened desiccated coconut
125 g/1 cup organic whole oats
125 g/1 cup plain/all-purpose flour
230 g/1 cup plus 2 tablespoons golden caster/natural cane sugar
125 g/1 stick unsalted butter
1 tablespoon golden syrup or runny honey
1 teaspoon bicarbonate of soda/baking soda

1–2 baking sheets lined with baking paper

Makes about 30 cookies

Preheat the oven to 180°C (350°F) Gas 4.

Put the coconut, oats, flour and sugar in a bowl and stir to combine. Make a well in the centre.

Put the butter, syrup or honey and 2 tablespoons cold water in a small saucepan and set over medium heat. Warm until the butter has melted and the mixture is just starting to bubble. Remove from the heat and stir in the bicarbonate of soda/baking soda. Pour this mixture into the dry ingredients and stir quickly until just combined.

Put teaspoons of the mixture onto the prepared baking sheets, leaving some space in between them. (You may need to cook the mixture in batches.) Bake in the preheated oven for about 10 minutes, until golden brown. Transfer to a rack to cool. Once cool, store in an airtight container and eat within 2–3 days.

wheat germ crisps with sesame seeds

These delicious crisp and buttery cookies have the added goodness of wheat germ, a tiny wheat seed that is extremely rich in proteins and vitamins. Wheat germ will only keep for a short period of time as its natural oil gradually becomes rancid stored at room temperature, so it should be kept in the fridge in an airtight container and used before the best-before date.

185 g/1 stick plus 4 tablespoons unsalted butter, at room temperature
185 g/¾ cup golden caster/natural cane sugar
1 egg, lightly beaten
25 g/3 tablespoons wheat germ
40 g/¼ cup sesame seeds
150 g/1 cup plus 2 tablespoons plain wholemeal/white whole-wheat flour
½ teaspoon baking powder

1–2 baking sheets lined with baking paper

Makes about 36 cookies

Preheat the oven to 180°C (350°F) Gas 4.

Beat the butter and sugar until pale and creamy. Add the egg and beat for 1 minute more. Fold in the wheat germ, sesame seeds, flour and baking powder until well combined.

Put teaspoons of the mixture onto the prepared baking sheets, leaving some space in between them. (You may need to cook the mixture in batches.) Bake in the preheated oven for 12–15 minutes, until golden and crisp. Transfer to a wire rack to cool. Once cool, store in an airtight container and eat within 2 days.

oaty biscuits

These simple biscuits are not overly sweet and make a good accompaniment to a full-flavoured cheese such as Parmesan, pecorino or mature Cheddar. If you can buy Spanish quince paste (membrillo) or any other fruit preserve, try serving this alongside.

165 g/1¼ cups rolled oats

50 g/¼ cup packed light soft brown sugar

200 g/1½ cups plain wholemeal/ whole-wheat flour

1 teaspoon bicarbonate of soda/baking soda

½ teaspoon sea salt

100 g/1 stick unsalted butter, melted

65 ml/¼ cup whole milk

1–2 baking sheets lined with baking paper

a 6-cm/2½ inch fluted cookie cutter

Makes about 36 biscuits

Preheat the oven to 180°C (350°F) Gas 4.

Put the oats and brown sugar in a mixing bowl and sift in the flour, bicarbonate of soda/baking soda and salt. Tip any husks from the sieve/strainer into the bowl.

Stir in the butter and milk to make a stiff dough. Briefly knead on a lightly floured work surface, then form into a ball and divide into two portions of equal size.

Roll each ball of dough out between two sheets of baking paper until no thicker than 2–3 mm/⅛ inch. Use the cutter to stamp out 18 biscuits from each portion of dough.

Arrange the biscuits on the prepared baking sheets and bake in the preheated oven for 12 minutes, until pale golden. Transfer to a wire rack to cool. Once cool, store in an airtight container and eat within 2–3 days.

Variation: To make a spiced fruit biscuit, add 50 g/2 oz. finely chopped dried apples or figs to the dry ingredients along with a pinch each of ground cinnamon and freshly grated nutmeg.

quinoa choc chip cookies

Although quinoa is most often used for stuffings, pilafs and baked dishes, it is also sometimes used for breakfast cereals, so, just like oats it makes a great addition to these home-baked biscuits. Use really good dark chocolate full of antioxidants to turn these into a guilt-free treat, packed with nutritious ingredients, that is far superior to any cookie you can buy.

60 g/½ cup rolled oats

150 g/¾ cup quinoa

125 g/1 cup plain/all-purpose flour

½ teaspoon baking powder

½ teaspoon bicarbonate of soda/baking soda

125 g/1 stick unsalted butter, at room temperature

100 g/½ cup demerara sugar

100 g/½ cup packed light soft brown sugar

1 egg

140 g/¾ cup roughly-chopped good quality dark or plain/bittersweet or semisweet chocolate, or chocolate chips

1–2 baking sheets lined with baking paper

Makes about 24 cookies

Preheat the oven to 180°C (350°F) Gas 4.

Put the oats and quinoa in a food processor and process until finely chopped and the mixture resembles ground almonds. Transfer to a bowl and add the flour, baking powder and bicarbonate of soda/baking soda. Mix to combine.

Put the butter and both sugars in a separate mixing bowl and beat for 4–5 minutes, until thick and pale. Add the egg and beat again briefly to combine. Stir in the dry ingredients to make a thick dough, then stir in the chopped chocolate or chocolate chips.

Put tablespoons of the mixture onto the prepared baking sheets and bake in the preheated oven for 10 minutes, until golden. Transfer to a wire rack to cool. Once cool, store in an airtight container and eat within 2–3 days.

maple, coconut and almond granola

This delicious granola can be enjoyed at breakfast time with fresh fruit and yogurt or as a nutritious snack. The cereal, nuts and grains added are all simply thrown together and baked until golden. The inclusion of something sticky such as sugar, honey or maple syrup as here, encourages the other ingredients to form themselves into moreish chewy and crunchy clumps.

375 g/2½ cups organic whole oats

1 tablespoon almond oil

30 g/¼ cup sunflower seeds

40 g/⅓ cup sesame seeds

25 g/3 tablespoons wheat germ

40 g/⅓ cup unsweetened desiccated coconut

30 g/¼ cup flaked almonds

3 tablespoons pure maple syrup

3 tablespoons light soft brown sugar, sifted

Makes 4–6 servings

Preheat the oven to 180°C (350°F) Gas 4.

Put the oats and almond oil in a small roasting pan and cook in the preheated oven for 20 minutes, stirring every 5 minutes.

Remove from the oven and add the sunflower seeds, sesame seeds and wheat germ. Return the pan to the oven and cook for 10 minutes more, stirring after 5 minutes.

Remove from the oven and add the coconut and almonds. Return to the oven and cook for 8–10 minutes more, until the coconut is golden, stirring after 5 minutes.

Stir in the maple syrup until well combined, then sprinkle over the brown sugar. Return to the oven and cook for 5 minutes more, until the granola is toasted and an even golden colour all over.

Let cool, then store in an airtight container for up to 5 days.

blueberry and apple muffins with bran

As I make muffins on a regular basis I really appreciate a recipe that is simple and quick. I like to use buttermilk but this can sometimes be tricky to find. Milk curdled with freshly squeezed lemon juice works just as well and frozen blueberries are a year-round treat. The most important thing to remember when following any muffin recipe is not to overmix. Use a large spoon to fold the ingredients together. You want it to look lumpy; if you end up with a smooth mixture it means your muffins will be tough.

250 ml/1 cup buttermilk (or 250 ml/ 1 cup whole milk soured with 1 tablespoon freshly squeezed lemon juice)

65 ml/¼ cup pure vegetable oil

375 g/3 cups plain/all-purpose flour

50 g/⅓ cup unsweetened bran cereal (such as All-bran)

1 generous tablespoon baking powder

1 small green eating apple, peeled, cored and grated

200 g/1⅓ cups fresh or frozen blueberries

1 egg

150 g/⅔ cup golden caster/natural cane sugar

butter or cream cheese, to serve

a 12-hole muffin pan, greased

Makes 12 muffins

Preheat the oven to 180°C (350°F) Gas 4.

Put the buttermilk in a jug/pitcher. Add the oil and stir well to combine.

Put the flour, bran cereal and baking powder in a mixing bowl and stir to combine. Add the grated apple and use your hands to combine the ingredients, separating the apple pieces and tossing to coat in the flour. Add the blueberries, and again use your hands to combine.

Put the egg and sugar in a separate bowl and whisk for 1 minute, until thick and pale. Add the buttermilk mixture and whisk to combine. Pour this into the dry ingredients and use a large metal spoon to gently fold together for a few seconds only, without overmixing.

Spoon the mixture into the prepared muffin pan, dividing evenly. Bake in the preheated oven for about 20 minutes, until risen and golden. Serve warm with butter or cream cheese. These are best eaten on the day they are baked.

easy banana bread

Think you can't bake? Well, you haven't tried this recipe. Make it on the morning you intend to eat it and fill the house with the seductive smell of cinnamon. Serve it warm spread with fresh ricotta and honey. Or make it a day or two in advance and lightly toast to serve.

200 g/¾ cup golden caster/natural cane sugar

2 eggs

125 ml/½ cup pure vegetable oil

2 bananas, peeled and mashed

260 g/2 cups plain wholemeal/white whole-wheat flour

1½ teaspoons baking powder

1 teaspoon ground cinnamon

fresh ricotta and honey, to serve (optional)

a 20 x 10 cm/8 x 4 inch loaf pan, greased

Makes 1 medium loaf

Preheat the oven to 180°C (350°F) Gas 4.

Whisk the sugar and eggs together in a bowl. Stir in the oil and 65 ml/¼ cup cold water until well combined.

Stir in the mashed bananas, flour, baking powder and cinnamon until just combined. Spoon into the prepared loaf pan and bake in the preheated oven for 50–55 minutes, until golden and firm on top. Let cool in the pan for 10 minutes before inverting onto a wire rack.

Serve warm on the day it is made or cooled and toasted, with ricotta and honey, if liked. The bread will keep for up to 2 days in an airtight container.

Variation: For a tasty banana and date bread, add 100 g/ 4 oz. chopped pitted dates to the mixture. This mixture also makes great muffins – just spoon the mixture into a greased 12-hole muffin pan and bake in a preheated oven at 180°C (350°F) Gas 4 for 20–25 minutes, until risen and golden. Drizzle over a little honey while the muffins are still warm.

four-flour bread

This wholesome bread is very therapeutic to prepare – just give yourself some time to enjoy the process and not feel rushed. It's very rewarding to make on a weekend morning to enjoy for lunch with a comforting soup.

500 g/3½ cups plain wholemeal/ whole-wheat flour

50 g/½ cup rye flour

50 g/½ cup spelt flour

50 g/½ cup soya flour

2 teaspoons sea salt

30 g/¼ cup organic whole oats

80 g/⅓ cup packed light soft brown sugar, plus 1 teaspoon

2 teaspoons dried yeast

65 ml/¼ cup rice bran oil

a 20 x 10 cm/8 x 4 inch loaf pan, lightly greased

Makes 1 medium loaf

Sift all four of the flours and salt into a large mixing bowl. Stir in any husks from the sieve/strainer, the oats and the 80 g/ ⅓ cup of sugar. Set aside.

Put the yeast and the 1 teaspoon of sugar in a small bowl and add 125 ml/½ cup warm water. Cover and set aside in a warm place for 10–15 minutes, until frothy and bubbling.

Add the yeast mixture, 375 ml/1½ cups warm water and the oil to the flour mixture and stir well to combine. Cover and set aside in a warm place for about 30–45 minutes, until just risen slightly.

Preheat the oven to 220°C (425°F) Gas 7.

Knead the dough on a lightly floured work surface for 8–10 minutes. Divide into two equal portions and form each into a ball. Sit each ball side by side in the prepared loaf pan. Cover and set aside in a warm place for 30 minutes. Lightly brush the top of the dough with water and bake in the preheated oven for 20 minutes. Reduce the temperature to 180°C (350°F) Gas 4 and bake for 20–25 minutes more, until risen and golden and the loaf sounds hollow when tapped on the base. This bread is best eaten on the day it is made.

chilli cornbread

This is great 'pan-baked' bread made using fine cornmeal. You could add the kernels from a cob of fresh sweetcorn too if liked, just stir them in after the eggs. I actually like to eat this for breakfast, toasted and served with scrambled eggs and chilli sauce on the side, but it's a great side with a chili con carne. This freezes well, simply reheat in the oven before serving.

225 g/1¾ cups fine yellow cornmeal

60 g/½ cup plain/all-purpose flour

1 teaspoon bicarbonate of soda/baking soda

2 teaspoons baking powder

1 teaspoon fine sea salt

1 teaspoon (caster) sugar

1 teaspoon dried chilli/hot pepper flakes

a handful of fresh coriander/cilantro leaves, roughly chopped

250 ml/1 cup buttermilk (or 250 ml/1 cup whole milk soured with 1 tablespoon freshly squeezed lemon juice)

65 ml/¼ cup single/light cream

80 g/8½ tablespoons unsalted butter

3 eggs, lightly beaten

a 20 x 30 cm/8 x 12 inch baking pan, greased and lined with baking paper

Makes about 16 pieces

Preheat the oven to 200°C (400°F) Gas 6.

Sift the cornmeal, flour, bicarbonate of soda/baking soda, baking powder and salt into a large mixing bowl. Stir in the chilli/hot pepper flakes and coriander/cilantro and make a well in the centre.

Put the buttermilk, cream and butter into a small saucepan and set over low heat. Heat until the butter has just melted. Pour into the flour mixture along with the beaten eggs, stir quickly to combine, then pour into the prepared baking pan.

Bake in the preheated oven for 18–20 minutes, until golden. Let cool in the pan for 5 minutes, then lift out and cut into squares. Keep covered with a clean napkin and serve while still warm.

couscous and cashew nut soda bread

This was something of an experiment but thankfully one with delicious results! Don't worry if the mixture looks a bit wet – as it cooks the couscous expands to give you a nutty loaf that's light, fluffy and easy to slice. Serve with dips, soups or alongside any grazing platter.

300 g/2½ cups plain wholemeal/
whole-wheat flour

1 teaspoon bicarbonate of
soda/baking soda

1 teaspoon baking powder

60 g/scant ½ cup couscous

100 g/⅔ cup salted cashew nuts,
roughly chopped

250 ml/1 cup buttermilk (or 250 ml/
1 cup whole milk soured with
1 tablespoon freshly squeezed
lemon juice)

*a 20 x 10 cm/8 x 4 inch loaf pan,
lightly greased with olive oil*

Makes about 16 pieces

Preheat the oven to 200°C (400°F) Gas 6.

Put the flour, bicarbonate of soda/baking soda, baking powder, couscous and cashews in a large mixing bowl, making a well in the centre.

Pour the buttermilk into the flour along with 435 ml/ 1¾ cups warm water and stir quickly to combine.

Spoon the mixture into the prepared loaf pan and bake in the preheated oven for 45 minutes, until risen and golden on top.

Let cool in the pan for 10–15 minutes before turning out. Slice and serve while still warm or serve cooled and toasted. The bread will keep for up to 2 days in an airtight container.

Lebanese rose and pistachio rice pudding

This less-traditional rice pudding makes use of the floral and heady rosewater, a much-loved ingredient in the Middle East – do go easy though, only a little is needed.

1 litre/4 cups whole milk
110 g/1 cup short grain white rice
220 g/1 cup caster/granulated sugar
1 egg yolk
2 tablespoons cornflour/cornstarch
1–2 teaspoons rosewater, to taste
65 ml/¼ cup double/heavy cream
½ teaspoon ground cinnamon
50 g/⅓ cup shelled unsalted pistachios, roughly chopped

Serves 4

Pour 65 ml/¼ cup of the milk into a mixing bowl and set aside until needed.

Combine the remaining milk, rice and sugar in a heavy-based saucepan and set over low/medium heat. Cook for about 45–50 minutes, stirring often, until the rice is just tender (ensuring that it does not catch on the bottom of the pan).

Add the egg yolk and cornflour/cornstarch to the reserved milk and whisk until smooth. Slowly stir about 65 ml/¼ cup of the hot rice mixture into the yolk mixture and then return this to the rice mixture. Stir to combine, until the rice mixture has thickened. Remove from the heat and stir in the rosewater.

Set aside to cool. Meanwhile, whip the cream until softly peaking. Fold it into the cooled rice mixture and sprinkle with the cinnamon and pistachios. Serve at room temperature.

vanilla rice pudding

This is a traditional English rice pudding which is slow-cooked and develops a lovely golden skin on top. For a simple variation, try adding a handful of sultanas/golden raisins and a pinch of freshly grated nutmeg.

1 vanilla pod/bean
1 litre/4 cups whole milk
125 ml/½ cup single/light cream
50 g/½ stick unsalted butter
75 g/⅓ cup golden caster/natural cane sugar
100 g/½ cup short grain white rice

a medium flameproof baking dish

Serves 4

Preheat the oven to 150°C (300°F) Gas 2.

Roll the vanilla pod/bean between the palms of your hand to soften. Split it lengthways with a small sharp knife and use the tip of the knife to scrape the seeds directly into a bowl. Add the milk, sugar and cream and whisk well to combine.

Put the butter in a medium, flameproof baking dish and set over high heat. When the butter is sizzling add the rice and stir for 1–2 minutes, until it is shiny and glossy. Carefully pour the milk mixture into the dish and use a large spoon to gently stir, breaking up any large lumps of rice and freeing any grains that are stuck to the bottom of the dish.

Transfer to the preheated oven and bake, uncovered, for 3 hours, until the top has a golden brown crust. Let cool slightly before serving.

chocolate and aduki bean paste fingers

Aduki beans are tiny, deep-red beans which have a sweet, nutty flavour and are more often used for sweet dishes than for savoury ones. In Japan they are cooked, puréed and mixed with sugar to make a paste which is used to fill cakes. It can be bought ready-made but making it fresh is very easy and it tastes much better. It's not tooth-achingly sweet and is light on the palate after a meal, or simply enjoyed with a cup of green tea.

4 sheets filo/phyllo pastry dough

65 g/4 tablespoons unsalted butter, melted

½ quantity of home-made aduki bean paste (see recipe below) or 150 g/½ cup ready-made sweet aduki bean paste

100 g/4 oz. good quality dark chocolate, grated

2 tablespoons icing/confectioners' sugar

aduki bean paste:

200 g/1 cup dried aduki beans

200 g/1 cup caster/granulated sugar

a pinch of fine sea salt

a baking sheet lined with baking paper

Makes about 8 fingers

To make the aduki bean paste, put the beans in a large, heavy-based saucepan and add enough cold water to cover them. Bring to the boil, then drain. Return the drained beans to the pan, add 750 ml/3 cups cold water and leave them to soak for 24 hours. (Discard any beans that remain floating.)

Bring the beans and soaking water to the boil, then reduce the heat and simmer for about 1 hour. Stir frequently with a wooden spoon until the beans are very soft and the water is almost absorbed. Add the sugar and stir. Add a pinch of salt, then transfer the beans to a food processor and blend to a smooth paste.

Preheat the oven to 220°C (425°F) Gas 7.

Cut each sheet of filo/phyllo in half lengthways so you are left with 8 pieces. Lay one of the pieces on a work surface and lightly brush all over with the melted butter.

Put about 2 generous teaspoons of the aduki bean paste in the centre of the filo/phyllo at the edge nearest you, making a mound about 5 cm/2 inches long. Sprinkle over some of the chocolate. Roll the filo/phyllo over to enclose the filling, fold in the sides and continue rolling to form a log. Repeat to make 8 logs.

Arrange the filo/phyllo fingers on the prepared baking sheet and bake in the preheated oven for 8–10 minutes, until golden and crisp. Dust lightly with icing/confectioners' sugar and serve warm.

little almond, polenta and lemon syrup cakes

Polenta is Italian cornmeal and it comes in various grades, ranging from coarse to fine – you want a very fine grade here (which you should be able to find at any Italian deli) for a good dense texture. It's best to eat these cakes on the day you make them, but that shouldn't be too difficult!

140 g/1 cup fine polenta

1 tablespoon baking powder

250 g/1¾ cups ground almonds

225 g/2 sticks unsalted butter, at room temperature

275 g/1 cup golden caster/natural cane sugar

1 tablespoon very finely grated lemon zest

4 eggs

lemon syrup:

115 g/½ cup golden caster/natural cane sugar

2 tablespoons freshly squeezed lemon juice

3 tablespoons flaked almonds, lightly toasted

icing/confectioners' sugar, to serve

a 12-hole muffin pan, lightly greased

Makes 12 cakes

Preheat the oven to 180°C (350°F) Gas 4.

Sift the polenta, baking powder and ground almonds into a large mixing bowl. Tip any pieces of husk into the bowl and make a well in the centre.

In a separate bowl, beat the butter, sugar and lemon zest together until pale and creamy. Add the eggs one at a time, beating well after each addition. Gradually fold in the polenta mixture until well combined.

Spoon the mixture into the prepared muffin pan, dividing evenly. Bake in the preheated oven for 25 minutes, until risen and golden. Remove from the oven and let cool in the pan for 10 minutes. Carefully transfer the cakes to a wire rack set over a baking sheet (to catch any drips of syrup later on).

To make the lemon syrup, put the sugar, lemon juice and 2 tablespoons cold water in a small saucepan. Set over low heat and cook, stirring, until the sugar dissolves. Increase the heat to high and bring to the boil, then reduce the heat to a low simmer and cook for 2–3 minutes, until syrupy.

Pour the syrup over the warm cakes. Sprinkle the flaked almonds on top so they stick to the syrup. Let cool and dust with icing/confectioners' sugar before serving.

home-made semolina crumpets

The raising agent in crumpets is yeast and when the batter is exposed to the heat of the frying pan, the air that is created by the yeast during its 'proving' expands and rises to the top of the crumpet, so they develop those distinctive little holes on top. These are densely textured crumpets and don't worry if the batter looks uncooked, as they are toasted before serving. Once upon a time you could buy specially-made crumpet rings but they are harder to find these days. Egg cooking rings do the job nicely but must be well greased before they are filled with batter.

125 g/1 cup strong plain bread flour

125 g/1 cup fine semolina

1 teaspoon golden caster/natural cane sugar

1 tablespoon dried yeast

about 50 g/½ stick unsalted butter, for cooking

to serve:

fruit jam and whipped cream, or butter and honey

4 egg cooking rings, each about 8–10 cm/3–4 inches diameter, well greased

Makes 8–10 crumpets

Put the flour, semolina, sugar and yeast in the goblet of a blender. With the motor running, add 325 ml/1⅓ cups warm water and continue to blend for 1 minute more. Scrape down the sides of the blender and blend for a further 30 seconds so the mixture is free of lumps. Pour into a large bowl, cover with clingfilm/plastic wrap and set aside in a warm place for 45–60 minutes, until the mixture is very frothy and bubbly.

Generously grease a heavy-based frying pan (or cast iron griddle pan if you have one) with butter and set over high heat. Sit the prepared egg cooking rings in the pan and ladle about 125 ml/½ cup of the crumpet mixture into each ring. Cook for 4–5 minutes, until bubbles form on the top and the sticky dough on the top has dried. Do not turn over. Transfer the cooked crumpets to a wire rack to cool and continue until all the batter has been used (regreasing the pan each time).

Preheat the grill/broiler to high. Lightly toast the tops of the crumpets, until golden. Serve hot with fruit jam and whipped cream, or butter and honey, as preferred.

oaty apple and raisin crumble

A baked fruit crumble, served warm from the oven, has to be one of the most popular comfort puds. And the good news is that compared to most other desserts it is a healthy choice! I think that oats are a must in any crumble topping as they make for a deliciously crunchy texture.

2 tablespoons brandy

1 tablespoon runny honey

50 g/⅓ cup raisins (preferably flame)

5 Granny Smith apples, peeled cored and sliced

75 g/½ cup golden caster/natural cane sugar

vanilla ice cream or chilled pouring cream, to serve

crumble topping:

75 g/⅔ cup plain wholemeal/whole-wheat flour

30 g/¼ cup rolled oats

½ teaspoon baking powder

½ teaspoon ground cinnamon

75 g/2 tablespoons unsalted butter, chilled and cut into cubes

60 g/5 tablespoons light soft brown or demerara sugar

a medium baking dish, buttered

Serves 4

Preheat the oven to 200°C (400°F) Gas 6.

Put the brandy, honey and raisins in a small saucepan and set over medium heat. Cook for 5 minutes, stirring constantly, until almost all the liquid has evaporated. Set aside.

Put the apples, sugar and 2 tablespoons cold water in a separate saucepan and set over medium heat. Cover and cook for 10–15 minutes, stirring often, until the apples have softened. Stir in the raisin mixture and let cool. Transfer to the prepared baking dish.

To make the crumble topping, put the flour, oats, baking powder, cinnamon and butter in a bowl. Use your hands to combine all of the ingredients, rubbing the butter between your fingertips, until the mixture resembles coarse sand. Stir in the brown sugar and sprinkle the mixture evenly over the apple mixture in the baking dish.

Bake in the preheated oven for 25–30 minutes, until the topping is crisp and golden. Serve warm with vanilla ice cream or chilled pouring cream, as preferred.

honeyed couscous with fresh figs and rosewater cream

In Morocco, sweet couscous is one of the most popular snacks and is also enjoyed as a nourishing breakfast, served with a variety of dried fruits and nuts and plenty of honey and cream for pouring. This is my take on the traditional recipe and makes a deliciously different and indulgent dessert.

140 g/1 cup couscous

1 tablespoon unsalted butter

2 tablespoons runny honey

½ teaspoon ground cinnamon

4–6 fresh figs, halved

1 teaspoon golden caster/natural cane sugar

125 ml/½ cup clotted or double/heavy cream

2 tablespoons light soft brown sugar

½ teaspoon rosewater

Serves 4

Put the couscous in a heatproof bowl and set aside.

Put the butter, honey, cinnamon and 125 ml/½ cup cold water in a small saucepan and set over high heat. As soon as the mixture boils pour it over the couscous, quickly stir just to combine and cover tightly with clingfilm/plastic wrap. Let sit for 10 minutes, then fluff up with a fork, making certain to pick up the grains at the bottom of the bowl. Re-cover and let sit for 5–10 minutes more. When cool enough to handle, use your fingertips to fluff and separate the grains for a light-as-air texture.

Preheat the grill/broiler to high. Sprinkle the golden caster/natural cane sugar over the cut sides of the figs and cook under the grill/broiler, until the sugar is golden and the figs have softened just slightly.

Put the cream, brown sugar and rosewater in a small bowl and stir to combine.

To serve, spoon the couscous into serving bowls, arrange a few fig halves on top and add a spoonful of the rosewater cream. Serve immediately.

spiced oatmeal cake with chocolate and cinnamon frosting

This is a dense and richly spiced cake and not one for the fainthearted. It is smothered with a finger-licking ganache of chocolate and cream which is good enough to eat on its own but do try and save some for the cake!

80 g/⅔ cup rolled oats

125 g/1 stick unsalted butter, at room temperature

115 g/½ cup packed light soft brown sugar

115 g/½ cup caster/granulated sugar

2 eggs

185 g/1⅓ cups plain/all-purpose flour

1 teaspoon baking powder

1 teaspoon ground cinnamon

¼ teaspoon freshly grated nutmeg

cinnamon chocolate frosting:

200 ml/¾ cup single/light cream

200 g/6 oz. premium dark chocolate, broken into small pieces

½ teaspoon ground cinnamon

a springform cake pan, 20 cm/ 8 inches diameter, lightly greased and lined with baking paper

Serves 10–12

Preheat the oven to 180°C (350°F) Gas 4.

Put the oats in a heatproof bowl. Add 300 ml/1¼ cups boiling water and stir. Cover with clingfilm/plastic wrap and let sit for 20 minutes.

Put the butter and both sugars in a mixing bowl and beat together until pale, thick and creamy.

Add one of the eggs and beat until well combined. Add the remaining egg and beat again. Stir in the flour, baking powder, cinnamon and nutmeg, then fold in the softened oats. Spoon the mixture into the prepared cake pan and level the surface.

Bake in the preheated oven for 35–40 minutes, until golden. Let cool in the pan for 10 minutes, then transfer to a wire rack to cool completely.

To make the frosting, set a heatproof bowl over a saucepan of barely simmering water, making certain the boiling water does not come into contact with the bottom of the bowl. Pour the cream into the bowl and let it warm slightly. Add the chocolate and cinnamon and stir constantly until the chocolate has melted and the mixture is dark and smooth.

Remove from the heat and let cool for about 30 minutes, until the frosting is a thick, spreading consistency. Use a palette knife or spatula to spread the frosting evenly over the sides and top of the cake. Cut into slices to serve. The cake will keep in an airtight container for 2–3 days.

index

aduki beans: chocolate and aduki bean paste fingers, 147
almonds: little almond, polenta and lemon syrup cakes, 148
Moroccan-spiced brown rice with currants and, 85
Anzac cookies, 129
apples: blueberry and apple muffins, 135
oaty apple and raisin crumble, 153
artichokes: lentil and artichoke salad, 71
aubergine (eggplant), chilli and cannellini bean salad, 67
avocado, Mexican taco salad with pinto beans and, 64

bacon, puy lentils with, 91
baked beans, smoked, 111
bananas, easy banana bread, 136
barley: barley and autumn vegetable soup, 50
barley risotto with mushrooms and goat's cheese, 120
fresh shiitake and barley soup, 50
lamb and vegetable soup with split peas and, 46
beef: Hungarian goulash, 108
real chili con carne, 111
biscuits (cookies): Anzac cookies, 129
oaty biscuits, 130
quinoa choc chip cookies, 131
wheat germ crisps with sesame seeds, 129
black beans: spicy chilli bean dip, 14
black-eyed bean and red pepper salad, 71
blueberry and apple muffins, 135
borlotti beans, heirloom tomato salad with mozzarella and, 61
bread: chilli cornbread, 140
couscous and cashew nut soda bread, 143
easy banana bread, 136
four-flour bread, 139
Spanish bread salad with chickpeas, chorizo and baby spinach, 63
broad beans (fava): bean, feta and dill salad, 55
bean and pork ragù, 100
falafel with minted yogurt, 22
ful medames, 13
Hungarian goulash with beans, 108

Moroccan bean and cumin dip, 13
pancetta and bean salad, 55
slow-cooked lamb salad with beans, 56
spicy three-bean salad, 59
buckwheat: buttered buckwheat with sweetcorn, 94
bulgur wheat: lamb kibbeh with garlic sauce, 29
butter beans: creamy curried parsnip and butter bean soup, 34
Greek salad with butter beans, 68
salt cod, potato and butter bean fritters, 25
three sisters soup, 33

cakes: blueberry and apple muffins 135
little almond, polenta and lemon syrup cakes, 148
spiced oatmeal cake, 157
cannellini beans: chicken, white bean and herb terrine, 26
chunky cannellini bean and tuna dip, 14
creamy cannellini, leek and sorrel soup, 41
herbed aubergine, chilli and cannellini bean salad, 67
hot smoked salmon and cannellini bean salad, 67
spicy three-bean salad, 59
Tuscan beans with fresh sage, 86
carrot and lentil dip, 13
cashew nuts: couscous and cashew nut soda bread, 143
cheese: barley risotto with mushrooms and goat's cheese, 120
bean, feta and dill salad, 55
black-eyed bean and red pepper salad with warm halloumi, 71
Greek salad with butter beans, 68
heirloom tomato salad with borlotti beans and mozzarella, 61
spiced pumpkin, spelt and goat's cheese salad, 76
chicken: chicken, white bean and herb terrine, 26
Chinese Hainan chicken rice, 124
poached chicken and brown rice salad, 75
roast chicken and chickpea

salad, 60
chickpeas: chickpea and fresh spinach curry, 115
chickpea pakoras with mango yogurt, 18
falafel with minted yogurt, 22
houmous, 17
Moroccan harira, 38
pasta e fagioli, 37
roast chicken and chickpea salad, 60
Spanish bread salad, 63
spiced chickpea and pumpkin fritters, 18
Chinese Hainan chicken rice, 124
chocolate: chocolate and aduki bean paste fingers, 147
quinoa choc chip cookies, 131
spiced oatmeal cake with chocolate and cinnamon frosting, 157
chorizo: smoky chorizo and bean soup, 41
Spanish bread salad with chickpeas, chorizo and baby spinach, 63
coconut: Anzac cookies, 129
maple, coconut and almond granola, 132
coconut milk: spicy coconut daal, 88
cod: salt cod, potato and butter bean fritters, 25
cookies see biscuits
corn see sweetcorn
cornbread, chilli, 140
couscous: couscous and cashew nut soda bread, 143
honeyed couscous with fresh figs and rosewater cream, 154
spiced buttered couscous, 94
crumble, oaty apple and raisin, 153
crumpets, semolina, 150
curries: chickpea and fresh spinach, 115
mung bean and vegetable, 119
prawn and yellow split pea, 116

daal, spicy coconut, 88
dips: carrot and lentil, 13
chunky cannellini bean and tuna, 14
Moroccan bean and cumin, 13
spicy chilli bean, 14
dolmades with green lentils, currants and herbs, 21

eggplant see aubergine
falafel with minted yogurt, 22

fava see broad beans
figs: honeyed couscous with fresh figs and rosewater cream, 154
ful medames, 13
fritters: spiced chickpea and, pumpkin, 18
salt cod, potato and butter bean, 25

garlic sauce, lamb kibbeh with, 29
ginger: Chinese Hainan chicken rice, 124
goulash: Hungarian goulash with beans, 108
granola, maple, coconut and oat, 132
Greek salad with butter beans, 68
green beans: three sisters soup, 33
gremolata, hot smoked salmon and cannellini bean salad with, 67

ham: pea and ham soup, 49
smoked baked beans, 111
haricot beans: pork sausage, fennel and haricot bean stew, 103
smoked baked beans, 111
smoky bean and lamb casserole, 105
smoky chorizo and haricot bean soup, 41
Tuscan beans, 86
houmous, 17
lemon and coriander/cilantro, 17
smoky paprika, 17
Hungarian goulash with beans, 108

Iranian rice, 92

kidney beans: real chili con carne, 111
Southern-style red beans and rice, 82
spicy three-bean salad, 59

lamb: lamb kibbeh with garlic sauce, 29
lamb and vegetable soup with split peas and barley, 46
Moroccan harira, 38
slow-cooked lamb salad with beans and pomegranate, 56
slow-cooked lamb shanks with lentils, 106
smoky bean and lamb

casserole, 105
Lebanese rose and pistachio rice pudding, 144
leeks: creamy cannellini, leek and sorrel soup, 41
lemon and cardamom basmati rice, 81
lentils: black lentils with lemon juice, 28
  brown lentil and Swiss chard soup, 45
  carrot and lentil dip, 13
  dolmades with green lentils, currants and herbs, 21
  ful medames, 13
  lentil and artichoke salad with salsa verde, 71
  Moroccan harira, 38
  mujaddarah, 88
  puy lentils with bacon, 91
  slow-cooked lamb shanks with lentils, 106
  spicy coconut daal, 88

Mexican taco salad with pinto beans and avocado, 64
Moroccan bean and cumin dip, 13
Moroccan harira, 38
Moroccan-spiced brown rice 85
mujaddarah, 88
mung bean and vegetable curry, 119
mushrooms: barley risotto with mushrooms and goat's cheese, 120
  fresh shiitake and barley soup, 50

oats: Anzac cookies, 129
  maple, coconut and almond granola, 132
  oaty apple and raisin crumble, 153
  oaty biscuits, 130
  spiced oatmeal cake, 157
olives: Greek salad with butter beans, 68

pakoras: chickpea pakoras with mango yogurt, 18
pancetta and bean salad, 55
parsnip: creamy curried parsnip and butter bean soup, 34
pasta: bean and pork ragù with tagliatelle, 100
  pasta e fagioli, 37
peas, split: lamb and vegetable soup with split peas and barley, 46
  pea and ham soup, 49
  prawn and yellow split pea curry, 116
pine nuts, baked inside-out stuffing with wild rice, sultanas and, 87

pinto beans: Mexican taco salad with avocado and, 64
  spicy pinto bean soup, 42
pistachio nuts: Lebanese rose and pistachio rice pudding, 144
polenta: little almond, polenta and lemon syrup cakes, 148
pomegranate, slow-cooked lamb salad with beans and, 56
pork: bean and pork ragù, 100
  pea and ham soup, 49
  slow-cooked pork belly with soya beans and miso, 99
  smoked baked beans, 111
potatoes: salt cod, potato and butter bean fritters, 25
prawns (shrimp): combination fried rice, 125
  prawn and yellow split pea curry, 116
pumpkin: spiced chickpea and pumpkin fritters, 18
  spiced pumpkin, spelt and goat's cheese salad, 76
pumpkin seeds, tamari brown rice with, 81

quinoa: quinoa choc chip cookies, 131
  quinoa, corn and tuna salad, 72
  quinoa tabbouleh, 72

rice: baked inside-out stuffing with wild rice, pine nuts and sultanas, 87
  barley risotto with mushrooms and goat's cheese, 120
  Chinese Hainan chicken rice, 124
  combination fried rice, 125
  dolmades with green lentils and currants, 21
  Iranian rice, 92
  lemon and cardamom basmati rice, 81
  Moroccan-spiced brown rice 85
  mujaddarah, 88
  poached chicken and brown rice salad with ginger and lime, 75
  simple tomato and basil risotto, 122
  Southern-style red beans and, 82
  tamari brown rice with pumpkin seeds, 81
  Vietnamese 'red' rice, 93
rice puddings: Lebanese rose and pistachio, 144
  vanilla, 144
risottos: barley risotto with mushrooms and goat's cheese, 120
  simple tomato and basil, 122

salads 54–77
  black-eyed bean and red pepper salad, 71
  bean, feta and dill salad, 55
  Greek salad with butter beans, 68
  heirloom tomato salad with borlotti beans and mozzarella, 61
  herbed aubergine, chilli and cannellini bean salad, 67
  hot smoked salmon and cannellini bean salad, 67
  lentil and artichoke salad with salsa verde, 71
  Mexican taco salad with pinto beans and avocado, 64
  pancetta and bean salad, 55
  poached chicken and brown rice salad with ginger and lime, 75
  quinoa, corn and tuna salad, 72
  quinoa tabbouleh, 72
  roast chicken and chickpea salad, 60
  slow-cooked lamb salad with beans and pomegranate, 56
  Spanish bread salad with chickpeas, chorizo and baby spinach, 63
  spiced pumpkin, spelt and goat's cheese salad, 76
  spicy three-bean salad, 59
salsa verde, lentil and artichoke salad with, 71
sausages: pork sausage, fennel and haricot bean stew, 103
scallions see spring onions
semolina crumpets, 150
sesame seeds, wheatgerm crisps with, 129
shrimp see prawns
smoked salmon and cannellini bean salad, 67
soda bread, couscous and cashew nut, 143
sorrel: creamy cannellini, leek and sorrel soup, 41
soups 32–51
  barley and autumn vegetable, 50
  brown lentil and Swiss chard, 45
  creamy cannellini, leek and sorrel, 41
  creamy curried parsnip and butter bean, 34
  fresh shiitake and barley, 50
  lamb and vegetable with split peas and barley, 46
  Moroccan harira, 38
  pasta e fagioli, 37
  pea and ham, 49
  smoky chorizo and bean, 41
  spicy pinto bean, 42
  three sisters, 33

Southern-style red beans and rice, 82
soya beans: slow-cooked pork belly with miso and, 99
  white fish, soya bean and baby carrot hot pot, 112
Spanish bread salad with chickpeas, chorizo and baby spinach, 63
spelt: spiced pumpkin, spelt and goat's cheese salad, 76
spinach: chickpea and fresh spinach curry, 115
  Spanish bread salad with chickpeas, chorizo and, 63
spring onions: Chinese Hainan chicken rice, 124
squash: three sisters soup, 33
sultanas (golden raisins), baked inside-out stuffing with wild rice, pine nuts and, 87
sweetcorn (corn): buttered buckwheat with, 94
  quinoa, corn and tuna salad, 72
  three sisters soup, 33
Swiss chard: brown lentil and Swiss chard soup, 45

tabbouleh, quinoa, 72
tamari brown rice with pumpkin seeds, 81
terrine, chicken and white bean, 26
three sisters soup, 33
tomatoes: Greek salad with butter beans, 68
  heirloom tomato salad with borlotti beans and mozzarella, 61
  pasta e fagioli, 37
  simple tomato and basil risotto, 122
  spicy pinto bean soup, 42
tuna: chunky cannellini bean and tuna dip, 14
  quinoa, corn and tuna salad, 72
Tuscan beans with sage, 86

vanilla rice pudding, 144
Vietnamese 'red' rice, 93
vine leaves: dolmades with green lentils, currants and herbs, 21

wheat germ: maple, coconut and almond granola, 132
  wheat germ crisps with sesame seeds, 129
wild rice: baked inside-out stuffing with wild rice, pine nuts and sultanas, 87